D0820700

The U.S. Economy in World War II

Columbia Studies in Business, Government, and Society
Eli Noam, General Editor

Columbia Studies in Business, Government, and Society:

The Impact of the Modern Corporation, ed. by Betty Bock, Harvey
    J. Goldschmid, Ira M. Millstein, and F. M. Scherer, 1984

Video Media Competition: Regulation, Economics, and Technology, ed. by Eli Noam, 1985

The U.S. Economy in World War II

Harold G. Vatter

Columbia University Press

New York   1985

Library of Congress Cataloging in Publication Data

Vatter, Harold G.
  The U.S. economy in World War II.

  Bibliography: p.
  Includes index.
  1. United States—Economic conditions—1918–1945.
  2. United States—Economic conditions—1945–
  3. United States—Economic policy—1933–1945.
  4. United States—Economic policy—1945–1960.   I. Title.
  HC106.4.V3   330.973'0917   85-7789
  ISBN 0-231-05768-7

Columbia University Press
New York   Guildford, Surrey
Copyright © 1985 Columbia University Press

Printed in the United States of America

For Joy Spalding

Contents

Preface

THE PRESENT BRIEF survey of the U.S. economy and economic policy in the World War II period should help to fill the gap in the existing economic literature on the great upheavals that spanned the years from 1939 to the first postwar recession of 1947–48. There are less than a handful of works that even approach generality. Examples of ones that do so are John R. Craf's 1947 narrative, A *Survey of the American Economy, 1940–1946,* the U.S. Budget Bureau's 1946 *United States at War,* and Eliot Janeway's 1951 *Struggle for Survival.*

There are, of course, numerous excellent special histories of the economic aspects of the wartime American experience, studies usually confined to the war years proper. For example, we are fortunate that the Roosevelt administration instigated a continuous record of wartime developments. As a result, the *Historical Reports on War Administration* provide us with a luxuriant store of detailed information contained in studies whose typical theoretical presumption is, as is the case with the discussion of administration in this volume, that the appropriate treatment of administration should encompass the treatment of economic developments.

There is no general work of which I am aware that (1) provides an interpretive presentation of overall economic change, government policy, and the administration of controls; (2) connects the major social concomitants with those changes; and (3) integrates the war years with the ongoing process of economic history—particularly the connections between the war experience and the great, immediate postwar reshaping process in the economy and the economy's relation to the federal government. These characterizations constitute the central organizational objectives of the present highly interpretive work. The interpretive element is constructed around the basic hypothesis that the war accelerated and crystallized the definitive establishment of the U.S. mixed economy, a historical process inaugurated by the Great Depression and the New Deal.

I am much indebted to several people at Portland State University for their careful and critical reading of various chapters or sections of the manuscript, particularly my colleagues Jim Heath, John Walker, and Helen Youngelson. Grateful acknowledgement of most helpful criticism is also extended to Richard Sasuly and to Professor Ellis Hawley, Department of History, University of Iowa. While the book is very much better than it would have been without their suggestions, I bear sole responsibility for errors, defects, and failure to follow criticisms they have generously offered.

For most of the gruelling work required for preparation of the manuscript I am immensely indebted in particular to Rosa Housman and Mitsie Shinoda.

Harold G. Vatter

Portland, Oregon, 1985

Chapter One

From Neutrality to Participation: A Prefatory Survey

The Isolationist Drag on Preparedness

ISOLATIONISM DOMINATED AMERICAN thinking and governmental policy long before the wartime era that began with the Japanese invasion of Manchuria in 1931. It prevailed until late in 1940 when Japan joined Germany and Italy to form the Rome-Berlin-Tokyo Axis. The nation that had never joined the League of Nations was a profascist neutral during the 1936–37 "civil" war of world fascist intervention against the Loyalist regime in Spain. Neutrality Acts passed during 1935–39 gave indirect, de facto assistance to the Axis powers. Roosevelt's "quarantine the aggressors" speech in October 1937 was still a voice crying in an isolationist wilderness. Less than a year later (in March and September 1938) the United States accepted the Nazi annexation of Austria and then the Czech Sudetenland. The seizure of the rest of Czechoslovakia in March 1939 evoked only a verbal slap on the wrist from the United States. Isolationism and neutralism were essentially pro-Axis, because the fascist powers were militarily the strongest, and the influence of these attitudes seriously delayed American preparedness for the inevitable World War II participation.

The tradition of isolationism and neutrality, however perilous its import in the years of fascist aggression, had a deep-rooted legitimacy in American society. For one thing, an oversold and misrepresented World War I had produced a justified public backlash of disillusionment with, and suspicion toward, European entanglements. The backlash kept the United States out of the League of Nations. In addition, many people believed that powerful business interests often had a nefarious and sinister stake in the promotion of balance-of-power alliances with various expansionist countries. This conviction was reinforced by the wide publicity given the hearings before a Senate committee under Gerald Nye of North Dakota investigating the involvement of munitions firms and bankers in World War I. The hearings extended over the years 1934–36, and extensively circulated such doctrines as the poorly supported notion projected by Senator Clark of Missouri, that the American export of munitions to the Allies "ultimately led us into war."[1] In the judgment of one authority, in the 1930s "a whole generation of Americans had persuaded themselves that participation in World War I had been an avoidable mistake, concluded that the Wall Street bankers and 'merchants of death' had cunningly sold the war to an unsuspecting nation, and naively dismissed unpleasant facts as propaganda."[2]

Also, there were strong currents of both jingoist Americanism and honest conservative nationalism in the culture, currents that fostered a go-it-alone policy. The populous Midwest in particular was an area of concentration combining German and Irish isolationist sentiment with a Progressive belief that involvement in the spreading global conflict would divert from and hamstring the domestic momentum toward social reform.[3] Within American society there were always present currents of antiwar sentiment, skepticism toward the obvious biases of public leaders, hopes that the foreign war would be temporary, and the tendency to rely on national security through the country's geographical insulation—what Selig Adler has aptly called "continental know-nothingism."[4]

The tide of sentiment began to turn in significant degree only with Hitler's march into Poland and the consequent declaration of war by

France and Britain in September 1939. (See the chronology in chart 1.1.) That year nonetheless still found the U.S. economy both overwhelmingly civilian and severely depressed. National defense expenditures of $1.24 billion in 1939 were only 1.4 percent of GNP, scarcely above the 1938 proportion. The average unemployment rate was over 17 percent, some 9½ million workers.

Nor did 1940 look very different. Articulate sentiment was still predominantly isolationist, and this was reflected in the state of the economy. The civilian labor force average annual unemployment rate fell only to about 15 percent. Real gross private domestic investment was still 18 percent below the 1929 prosperity level. Real cash receipts from farm marketings were only 15 percent, industrial production only 16 percent, above 1929. That year therefore also belongs to the depression decade in the economic sense. The military economy that finally cured the depression had not yet taken hold, although the transformation of public opinion and administrative policy necessary for conversion to a war economy did seriously commence during 1940. That year and the first half of 1941 constituted an eighteen-month period during which the vision of inevitable American participation gradually came to replace the abhorrence toward involvement.

Perhaps the supercession of civilian by military economy should be dated roughly with the passage of the March 1941, "arsenal of democracy," Lend-Lease Act. That legislation authorized the President to supply military or other goods to any country whose interests were deemed vital to the defense of the United States. In the first year under Lend-Lease approximately $112 billion in aid was granted, most of it, of course, to Great Britain.

The struggle of the prodemocratic "premature antifascist" groups supporting France, Britain, and their allies was not an easy one. Isolationist elements in Congress were very strong right up to December 7, 1941. As late as the 1940 presidential election campaign, President Roosevelt's representation of himself as strongly anti-Hitler and anti-isolationist was minimally, almost blatantly, deceptive. However, he had already timorously committed himself and his administration to a stance similar to that of the Committee to Defend America by Aiding the Allies, established in June 1940. Various mincing administrative and legislative moves had been made even in 1939. These included

Chart 1.1
Chronology of Main War Events Before
Pearl Harbor (December 7, 1941)

1931   Japan invades Manchuria (December).

1933   Japan invades the five northern provinces of China.

1935   Nazis take over Rhineland (Versailles Treaty buffer zone).

1936   Second Neutrality Act forbids all loans to belligerents.
        Formation of Rome-Berlin Axis alliance.
        Italy conquers Ethiopia.

1937   German and Italian intervention in Spanish civil war.
        Italy joins Germany and Japan in anti-Comintern pact.
        Full-scale extension of Sino-Japanese War.
        Third Neutrality Act continues embargo on finished munitions, gives President
           authority to sell munitions to any belligerent on cash-and-carry basis, i.e., no
           aggressor/belligerent distinction.
        President makes famous October "quarantine the aggressors" speech.
        Mild U.S. rebuke to Japan for sinking American gunboat *Panay*.

1938   Nazis invade and annex Austria.
        Nazis occupy Czech Sudetenland.
        British fleet put on war alert in September.

1939   Nazis conquer remainder of Czechoslovakia.
        Hungary occupies Ruthenia (a province of Czechoslovakia).
        Lithuania cedes seaport of Memel to Germany.
        Italy invades Albania.
        Formalization of Rome-Berlin alliance in "Pact of Steel."
        Nazi-Soviet nonaggression pact (August).
        Nazis invade and conquer Poland (September 1); Poland partitioned by Germany,
           USSR.
        Britain and France declare war on Germany (September 3); U.S. proclaims neu-
           trality.
        U.S. lifts arms embargo, but reactivates cash-and-carry limitation as part of the
           Neutrality Act of 1939.
        German and Italian aid to Franco helps destroy Spanish Popular Front govern-
           ment; Fascists under Francisco Franco take power.
        August 2 letter of Albert Einstein delivered to President Roosevelt in October
           inaugurates atomic bomb ("Manhattan") project.
        Period of lull in European war theater ("Phony War"): October 1939–April 1940.
        Finnish-USSR war breaks out (November–December).
        U.S. accepts orders from Britain and France for 4,700 aircraft, costing $614
           million.[a]

[a] William L. Shirer, *The Collapse of the Third Republic* (New York: Simon and Schuster, 1969), p. 619*n*.

1940   Finnish-USSR war ends (March).

Nazi blitzkrieg in Europe (April 9–June 22): Denmark (possessor of Greenland), Norway, Netherlands (possessor of Dutch West and East Indies), Belgium, Luxembourg, France conquered.

British driven from foothold in Western Europe (massive evacuation from Dunkirk).

Italy declares war on Britain, France.

Fall of France (June).

USSR occupies Lithuania, Latvia, Estonia.

Declaration of Havana: Pan-American Ministers agree any attack on "American" country would be attack on all (July).

U.S. Congress implements two-ocean navy authorized by Naval Expansion Act of 1938, raising warship tonnage by 70 percent. President asks Congress for 50,000 airplanes a year (May).

Great air battles over England, devastation of British merchant fleet (summer).

Japanese invasion of Indo-China (September).

Formation of Berlin-Rome-Tokyo Axis alliance (Tripartite Pact; September).

Transfer of 50 over-age destroyers to Britain.

U.S. Selective Service Act (draft) passed.

Italy invades Greece.

1941   Bulgaria joins Axis alliance.

Passage of U.S. Lend-Lease Act.

Nazis occupy Greece, Yugoslavia.

U.S. occupies Greenland (April).

President Roosevelt declares state of unlimited national emergency (May).

Nazis invade USSR (June).

U.S. occupies Iceland, Trinidad, British Guiana.

Japan occupies all of Indo-China (July).

Closure of Panama Canal to Japanese shipping.

Japanese assets in United States frozen.

Extension of U.S. Selective Service law (August). Vote in House of Representatives, 203–202.

President Roosevelt orders U.S. navy to fire upon German and Italian naval vessels in North Atlantic (September).

U.S. Congress repeals 1939 Neutrality Act, authorizes arming of merchant vessels, and permits them to carry cargoes to belligerent ports.

the Strategic Materials Act of June 7 in that year, to stock critical materials "for defense," albeit at a woefully underfinanced pace.[5] Ineffectual administrative bodies were also set up, such as the War Resources Board (August 1939).[6] More immediately important for U.S. involvement and for isolating the isolationists, late in the year (November) the administration successfully engineered amendment of the Neutrality Acts to permit cash-and-carry munitions and arms sales to the belligerents, giving de facto arms aid thereby only to Britain and

France, since they alone had the necessary shipping and their navies could prevent Axis ships from getting through.

Involvement on the administrative policy level, if not yet substantial in military expenditures, was extensive. It moved at a somewhat faster pace after the variously dubbed "winter of waiting," "sitzkrieg," or "phony war" during the winter of 1939–40 ended, and Hitler launched his blitzkrieg in the spring and summer of 1940. In the early months of that year the President asked Congress for about $4 billion for national defense and for the inauguration of a two-ocean navy. However, actual national defense outlays rose only from $1.2 billion in 1939 to $2.2 billion—in a GNP of $100 billion—in 1940. (See chart 1.2.)

The early phases of economic mobilization, as reviewed in the First Annual Report of the Truman Committee,[7] were marked by frequent exploitation of the cost-plus-fixed-fee defense contract with the government; large tax concessions to business; business reluctance to let defense work interfere with hoarding of labor, equipment, and supplies and with ordinary, now-expanding markets; great regional concentration of defense contracts; and neglect of small business in the allocation of defense work (the arrangement whereby large firms subcontracted work to small hardly existed yet). There was also widespread reluctance (e.g., by the steel and aluminum industries) to expand capacity even at government expense, poor coordination of domestic civilian and military requirements with aid to Britain, too much autonomy for the armed services regarding priorities and procurement, and a generally profound underestimation of the magnitude of the defense task.

Following the capitulation of the Netherlands and Belgium, France fell to the Nazis in June 1940. In that same month a National Roster of Scientific and Specialized Personnel was established, a prophetic coincidence, for that personnel pool later fed many highly trained people to the atomic bomb project,[8] a historic endeavor for which Roosevelt, reacting to knowledge of German atomic research and the urges of Albert Einstein and others, had already committed some federal money in the fall of 1939. In August 1940 a Defense Plant Corporation to construct defense facilities was given access to funds from the Reconstruction Finance Corporation (RFC). The Hoover-created RFC (1932–56) subsequently played an important financing role for a number of wartime agencies. Then in September, following the Battle of Britain, the President declared a state of "limited national emergency" (made unlimited in May 1941),[9] and the Selective Service and Training Act, the nation's first peacetime draft law, was passed, anticipating a 1,200,000 man army and 800,000 reserves. Indeed, it was a memorable month, for September also saw the formation of the Rome-Berlin-Tokyo Axis and the fateful deal between the President and British Prime Minister Winston Churchill to transfer 50 obsolete U.S. destroyers to Britain in exchange for 99-year leases to the United States of a number of British military bases.

End of the Great Depression

Nevertheless, 1940 was the eleventh year of the Great Depression. No one can say for certain what would have been the future course of the civilian economic recovery following the cyclical trough of June 1938. On an annual basis, real GNP (in 1958 dollars) in 1940 was 17.6 percent above the 1938 trough. But this two-year recovery performance brought GNP to a level only 12 percent above the weak "peak" of 1937. Viewed in a longer perspective, 1940 real GNP was still only 9 percent above 1929. This was a historically miserable performance, particularly if one were to allow for some stimulus to the 1940 GNP level from business anticipations of a forthcoming preparedness boom (for example, there was a big jump in business civilian inventory investment in 1940). The value of the gross stock of business plant and equipment in 1940 was still slightly below what it had been in 1926![10] Even with a rising capacity/capital stock ratio, it is hard to believe that the expansion of the late 1920s had so overbuilt the nation's fixed capital stock that it would not ordinarily have been worked off long before 1940. It is noteworthy that the volume of real business fixed nonresidential investment in 1940 was still no higher than it had been in 1937, and was of course well below 1929 levels.

With a sharply falling government budget deficit in 1940[11] and a civilian unemployment rate of 14.6 percent, the economy was still far from promising to absorb fully that army of unemployed. In the con-

Chart 1.2
Highlights of U.S. Government
Economic Involvement Before
Pearl Harbor

1939: Anticipations

Year	
1939	Through implementation of contracts initiated in 1938, 440 American warplanes delivered and ready for action in France by May 1940; by June, 544 warplanes.[a]
June	Strategic Materials Act authorized appropriation of $100 million through June 30, 1943, to acquire and stockpile defense-critical materials. Initial appropriation: $10 million. The Reconstruction Finance Corporation Act of 1933 amended to permit establishment of subsidiary corporations (e.g., Metals Reserve Co., Defense Plant Corporation) to produce, or otherwise procure either domestically or through importation, and to store, "strategic materials."
	Initial implementation of 1938 Educational Orders Act, which had authorized substantial outlays to educate private, potential military suppliers regarding the War Department's technical specifications.
July	U.S. informs Japan that the 1911 commercial treaty would be unilaterally terminated in six months.
August	President appoints a War Resources Board to evaluate Industrial Mobilization Plan.
Fall	Commitment of federal seed money to atomic energy bomb project.
	Civil Aeronautics Agency between September 1939 and December 1941 teaches 60,000 college students how to fly.[b]
November	Lifting of the arms embargo against the Allies (through a new Neutrality law allowing sale of contraband on a cash-and-carry basis).

[a] William L. Shirer, *The Collapse of the Third Republic* (New York: Simon and Schuster, 1969), p. 619 *n*. Shirer provides no source reference for this information.
[b] Geoffrey Perrett, *Days of Sadness, Years of Triumph* (Baltimore: Penguin Books, 1974), p. 116.

1940: Guns and butter too

Expansion of commitment to the military, fiscal years ending June 30, 1939–1942		
	Outlays for army and navy (billions of dollars)	Military personnel on active duty (thousands, as of June 30)
1939	$1.4	334
1940	1.8	458
1941	6.3	1,801
1942	22.9	3,859

May	President asks Congress to appropriate an additional $900 million for the armed forces, 50,000 airplanes a year, and a two-ocean navy. Appoints a National Defense Advisory Commission to advise him on mobilization.

June	Revenue Act. Income tax exemptions lowered drastically. "Defense taxes" instituted: surtaxes, corporation income tax, personal income tax rates, and excise taxes are all increased. Total tax-yield rise: $1 billion. National debt ceiling raised.
	President sells $362 million of surplus war materials to Britain.
	Pittman Resolution authorizes sale of munitions to Latin-American countries.
	Congress moves to authorize acquisition of strategic raw materials and passes first Priorities Act giving preference to military orders.
July	Congress votes $5 billion for army and navy; authorizes $4 billion of national defense obligations—in excess of existing debt ceiling.
	Congress passes Export Embargo Act, authorizing the President to curtail or prohibit exports of any military or military-related supplies. Exports of steel and scrap iron prohibited.
September	One-year Selective Service law passed; the first peacetime draft in U.S. history.
	Fifty overage destroyers "traded" to Britain in exchange for naval and air bases.
	President declares "state of limited national emergency."
	Ban on sale of scrap iron to Japan; embargo on machine tools.
October	Revenue Act. Imposed excess profits tax, 25%–50%; increased normal corporation tax on net income greater than $25,000. Permitted corporations to write off investments in defense facilities at a rate of 20% per year for 5 years; they could thus amortize new plant and equipment out of defense profits and hold up-to-date facilities in peacetime following a possible war.
November	Inauguration of program to send one-half of all U.S. airplane production to Britain.

1941: Year of commitment and preparation

	Calendar year federal purchases of goods and services for national defense	
	purchases (billions of dollars)	in ratio to GNP (%)
1939	1.2	1.32
1940	2.2	2.20
1941	13.7	11.02
1942	49.4	31.17

Year 1941	Continued high sensitivity to adverse effects upon the unemployment rate of conversion to military production.
	Gradual encroachment of military demands upon "nonessential" civilian production:
	—some curtailment of civilian production
	—imposition of inventory ceilings (to forestall hoarding)
	—restrictions on uses to which some materials could be put.
	however:
	passenger car output, July 31, 1940 to July 31, 1941 was largest ever.

Chart 1.2—Continued
Highlights of U.S. Government
Economic Involvement Before
Pearl Harbor

1939: Anticipations

	All consumer durables expenditures (1972 dollars):	
	total real outlays (billions of dollars)	in ratio to GNP (%)
1939	19.1	5.97
1940	21.8	6.34
1941	24.7	6.23
1942	16.3	3.59

January	President's budget message calls for $11 billion for national defense.
	Creation of Office of Production Management (OPM) within Office of Emergency Management (OEM).
March	Lend-Lease Act passes Congress, authorizing the President to provide any article of defense to any country he deems vital to U.S. defense. $7 billion initial appropriation.
	Repair of British ships in U.S. yards authorized.
	OPM announces need for great expansion of nation's production capacity, and estimates total defense costs through 1942 to be $49 billion.
	National Defense Mediation Board established to deal with industrial disputes in defense sector.
April	Office of Price Administration and Civilian Supply created.
May	President declares state of unlimited national emergency.
June	Inauguration of "Victory Program" entailing a series of appropriations acts for military establishments and matériel.
July	Japanese assets in U.S. frozen and oil shipments embargoed.
	Decision to add USSR to Lend-Lease program.
August	Federal Reserve Board authorized to regulate installment buying.
	Establishment of Supply Priorities and Allocations Board.
	Extension of draft for 18 months.
September	Revenue Act. Personal exemptions again reduced, income and corporation and excess profits, tax rates increased. Makes numerous "temporary" excises permanent.
November	Federal Reserve Board increases reserve requirements to maximum allowable.

current absence of a significant rise in all government spending, the Keynesian proponents of a long-run growth retardation hypothesis would seem to have enjoyed strong empirical support in their controversy with other interpreters of the unusual duration of the Great Depression. It became a commonplace to observe that it required much more massive doses of Keynesian medicine (injections of big G) than had ever been applied by the civilian New Deal in order to finally bring full employment. And equally important, big government expenditures apparently had thereafter to be maintained if the mixed economy was to avoid severe depression. Of course, Keynesian medicine was prescribed for a condition of depression. It was not designed either for an economy experiencing exhilaration or for a host of related supply phenomena that cried out for social treatment during the decades following World War II.

Inauguration of War Economy

The effective beginning year of the military economy was 1941, particularly the latter half. It now seems almost incredible that this was a whole year after the fall of France and many months after the onset of the Battle of Britain. On the international political and military-strategic front, as well as on the domestic administrative and preparedness front, there was at last portentous activity. Fortunately, this activity antedated the Japanese Pearl Harbor attack on December 7. Indeed, by that time the nation was practically already at war.

On an annual basis, the first year of transition to a war economy was 1941. "Transition" because certain features of the peacetime depression still clung to 1941, and because the civilian economy continued to compete strongly with the oncoming wartime demands upon resources. With respect to the first aspect, for example, there was still a high 10 percent unemployment rate. Real gross private domestic investment was exactly equal to the 1929 level. Regarding the second aspect, real personal consumption, which had risen 5.1 percent in 1940, increased even more, by 6.2 percent, in 1941 (in the next year it fell absolutely). Domestic investment, still overwhelmingly civilian, also increased 26 percent in 1941 over 1940 (whereas it fell by almost one-half in the ensuing war year).

As noted earlier, military expenditures were slow to gain momentum. In the first half of 1941 the quarterly totals (at annual rates) were well below the annual rate; only in the third and fourth quarters were they well above it.[12] Thus the competition between civilian and military demand was very easy on the former during the first half of the year, but the military gradually began to crowd out the civilian during the latter half. This is indicated by the dropping off of durable consumer goods outlays in the third quarter, and of private domestic investment in the fourth quarter.

The best illustration of the mounting clash of civilian with military demands for durable goods as ominous 1941 plunged onward, and one of the dramatic events of the war period, was the controversy over the policy issues embodied in the Reuther plan for converting the motor vehicle industry. Walter Reuther was a maverick vice-president of the five-year-old United Auto Workers (UAW) when he proposed in December 1940 his blueprint for converting the excess capacity of the industry, which he estimated at a huge 50 percent, to the production of military aircraft. In advancing his proposal he not only symbolized labor's wartime dedication to the country's cause but was generally quite correct in practical terms. The motor vehicle industry, with some new plants and equipment, did eventually produce, in partial conjunction with the aircraft industry, a large volume of aircraft and parts. But almost equally important, Reuther called public attention to the critical impending shortage of machine tools, to say nothing of basic industrial materials, by including in his proposal the stipulation that the motor vehicle manufacturers relinquish their annual model change in 1941 in order to conserve machine tools.[13] He also thus precipitated the issue of labor training and utilization for war by urging that the 12,000 to 15,000 skilled mechanics released by the suggested model-change moratorium be employed in helping build the tools, dies, jigs, and other equipment necessary for the production of an all-metal fighter plane on a mass production schedule.[14]

Reuther brought into public focus an idea that had shortly before been anticipated to some extent by General Motors' William S. Knudsen, then a member of the powerless National Defense Advisory Commission, in charge of industrial production for defense.[15] But automobile management, like steel management and others, had its eye on favorable civilian market prospects, and had targeted sales of 4,000,000 cars for 1941, a goal it almost achieved.

Meanwhile, it had begun to produce military vehicles in quantity. But it viewed general curtailment and conversion as twin barriers to a profitable year, claiming that no more than 15 percent of its machine tools were convertible. The controversy over autos as well as other consumer durables was resolved only by the steel shortage and, ultimately, Pearl Harbor.[16] Only 223,000 passenger cars were produced (factory sales) in 1942, many for military use. Thereafter output was negligible until 1946.

In addition to the production of tanks, jeeps, and trucks during the war, the motor vehicle manufacturers were

the largest single group of suppliers to the aircraft manufacturers. They produced over $11 billion worth of aircraft, subassemblies, and parts, or 38.7 per cent of the dollar value of all military production by the automotive industry. They built 455,522 aircraft engines out of a total of 812,615 and 255,518 propellers out of 713,717 . . . Automobile companies also made some 27,000 complete aircraft (including helicopters and gliders).[17]

The last figure may be appreciated in the light of the fact that about 300,000 airplanes were produced during the war years. Reuther may have been wrong about the capacity of the motor vehicle industry to mass-produce complete aircraft, but his vision of a strategic role for the industry in military aircraft, and the necessity for conversion in 1941, was essentially correct.

We can date the cessation of high-level wartime economic effort approximately with the third quarter of 1945, when the quarterly total (at annual rates) of federal was expenditures fell below the huge grand total of $76.2 billion for that year. (The highest quarterly outlay, incidentally, was during the first quarter of 1945: over $92 billion at annual rates, which was almost 42 percent of total output.) Significantly, private fixed investment in the very next quarter rose sharply above the 1945 first-quarter level: victory in Europe (V-E Day) came on May 8, victory over Japan (V-J Day) on August 14, in 1945.

Hence, the period of all-out war economy spanned about four long years. However, the level of military expenditures even in the last quarter of 1945 was still high, at 25 percent of GNP—much above 1941's last quarter, at 16 percent.[18]

But 16 percent already represented a comparatively huge volume of Keynesian antidepression medicine. In the year 1939 total federal expenditures had been only 5.6 percent of GNP, and in 1940 they were 6 percent. As for the federal deficit, in ratio to GNP it was twice as high in 1941 as it had been in 1939. Hence, only the onset of war brought into operation Keynesian deficit spending of sufficient magnitude to end twelve years of mass unemployment. The necessary social consensus to accomplish that in the face of opposition by the dominant small budget balancers could not be crystallized then under civilian conditions. Indeed, as is well known, military and related expenditures continued to be the overwhelmingly preponderant component of the historically large federal outlays for goods and services throughout all the post–World War II decades. Criticism of those large expenditures was almost always leveled at the much smaller civilian portion, and at the public transfer payments to persons, although often not selected out and labeled as such. The American consensus never accepted a full-bodied, Keynesian *civilian* deficit-spending policy for maintaining high employment. And it never accepted ideologically the de facto, chronic federal deficits that stubbornly persisted year after year. Even as late as the 1980s a majority favored a federal constitutional amendment *to require an annually balanced budget*, and only a small percent had no opinion.

It is widely believed that the large army of unemployed and the attendant excess capacity in industry facilitated rapid conversion to a war economy in 1941 and 1942. There is considerable truth to this. However, except in raw materials, what was more urgently needed for defense production was retooling, revamping, and coordinating, rather than merely stepping up the rate of production and squeezing out excess capacity. In many lines of production conversion was an agonizing task.

It was also frequently boasted that the "arsenal of democracy" performed a miracle in outproducing the Axis soon after entering the war. One writer, for example, has noted the "six months after Pearl Harbor [the United States] had turned back the Japanese in the Pacific, while at home its factories were producing more than all the factories of the Axis nations put together."[19] While American production did rise dramatically, such comparisons frequently overlooked the high level of U.S. output even in a peacetime global context. Even in the recession year 1938, for example, the U.S. national income of $67.4 billion was almost twice the combined national income of Germany, Italy, and Japan.[20] The U.S. industrial production index (1947–49) in 1942 was 22 percent above the 1941 level, a noteworthy but distinctively smaller rise, in percentage terms, than "civilian" 1941 over 1940.[21] For the two-year period 1940–42, the certainly substantial 58 percent increase in the industrial production index may be compared with the cyclical recovery in the index of manufacturing production of 50 percent in peacetime from 1921 to 1923.[22]

One way of tracking the course of the war economy is to observe the declining percentage increases in the industrial production index after 1940–41:

1940–41	29.9%
1941–42	21.8
1942–43	19.8
1943–44	−1.6
1944–45	−14.4

These figures show that after 1943 industrial production, while remaining very great for at least another year, had begun to contract. (See chart 1.3.) Of course, the military component in 1944 was only slightly below that in 1943. A roughly similar pattern was traced by military goods purchases of the federal government, with the big percentage increase coming in 1940–41, proportionate declines thereafter, only a 5 percent rise in 1944, and a sharp absolute and relative drop in 1945. Still, such purchases totaled $51 billion in 1945—almost a fourth of GNP!

Employment Expansion, Productivity, and Labor Power

These great wartime production increases were attained primarily by employing more labor in combination with more energy and raw

Chart 1.3
Industrial Production
SOURCE: U.S., Bureau of the Budget, *The United States at War* (Washington, D.C.: GPO, 1946), p. 104.

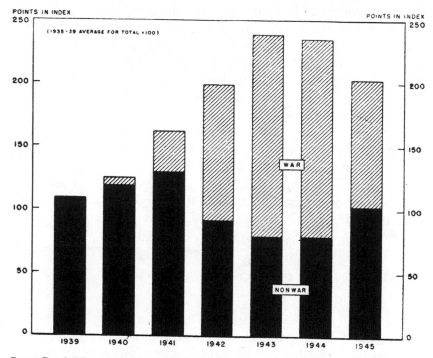

POINTS IN INDEX
250

(1935-39 AVERAGE FOR TOTAL =100)

200

150

WAR

100

50

NON WAR

0

1939   1940   1941   1942   1943   1944   1945

POINTS IN INDEX
250

200

150

100

50

0

Source: Board of Governors of the Federal Reserve System.

materials inputs, but with very moderate additions to the preexisting capital stock (which, of course, was underutilized in 1940). The civilian labor input increases were a combination of more employed nonagricultural workers and longer hours.

Looking at the private "civilian" sector that produced both civilian products and military commodities, employment rose by about five million, or almost 12 percent, between 1940 and the 1943 wartime employment peak. But total private civilian *labor hours* also increased. Average weekly hours worked by manufacturing production workers, to take as an example perhaps the largest sectoral percentage rise,[23] increased from a depression-lingering 38.1 in 1940 to about 45 in both 1943 and 1944—the same as they had been far back in peacetime

1926 before the 40-hour work week became established (beginning in 1946). The President's Executive Order of February 9, 1943, establishing a minimum work week of 48 hours, was generally not observed outside Class I railroads and certain critically short of labor activities.

But the federal government made even greater demands upon the adult population for more labor power. Indeed, it added over 12 million persons to its payroll over that short span of war years, 1941–45: almost 2 million to the Department of Defense and other regular agencies, plus well over 10 million to the armed forces.[24]

Where did this huge additional prime-age human contingent of about 17 million come from? About 10 million represented new entrants into the nation's total civilian labor and military forces, over one-half of whom were civilian women.[25] About 7 million of the contingent come from the unemployed ranks. In this respect the large pool of unemployed inherited from the depression was decisive, for over the period 1940–43 unemployment declined from over 8 million to about 1 million, even as the civilian labor force held constant at about 56 million.

Many hundreds of thousands of the new civilian labor force recruits, as well as recruits for the armed forces, must have come from agriculture, because that sector was harboring disguised unemployed as well as officially unemployed people in 1940. The farm population in 1940 was as large as it had been in 1930, even though the number of employed persons in farming was 800,000 less than it had been in 1930, and agricultural gross product was about 9 percent higher in 1940 than ten years previously (indicating a rise in employed labor productivity). Only about 600,000 persons transferred out of farm *employment* between 1940 and 1944, but the total farm *population* fell by 5.7 million. With a farm labor participation rate (labor/population) of about one-third, clearly agriculture, despite its critical-industry, draft-deferred status, contributed well over a million and a quarter additional people to the civilian labor force and/or the armed forces from the "surplus" population of working age as of 1940.

But the problems of wartime labor supply were vastly more complicated than augmentation of the total. It was necessary to recruit and place workers in accordance with a system of industrial, occupational, and spatial priorities. Training of the unskilled and unadapted worker for specific war-industry tasks had to be undertaken, and specific labor shortages overcome. Occupational deferments from military service were widely instituted. New housing and child care facilities had to be provided in cities of war production concentration, especially on the West Coast. Steps had to be taken to avoid labor pirating and hoarding, high absenteeism and turnover, wasteful migration, and discrimination against minorities and women. It is revealing of the prejudice against women that the President's June 1941 Executive Order no. 9346 creating the Fair Employment Practices Committee (FEPC) stipulated race, creed, color, and national origin, but omitted sex—despite the nation's enormous reliance upon womanpower.

Output expansion for war, and to a small degree likewise for the civilian sector, was also aided by productivity rise over the years 1940–44. The sum of civilian production and military commodities purchased by the federal government rose 52 percent;[26] hence civilian "labor productivity" (that sum divided by private civilian labor hours)[27] increased by about 27 percent.

Total production expansion was also fostered by an accompanying 30 percent increase in output per unit of capital input in the total economy.[28] Again, depression excess capacity, when converted, helped expedite the military buildup.[29] But capital productivity was also abetted by two-shift and even round-the-clock operation in many cases.

We may again fruitfully compare the wartime total-factor productivity record (TFP—output rise relative to the rise in all inputs) with that for the peacetime cyclical expansion of the early 1920s. At the bottom of the 1920s' recession in 1921, the unemployment rate was 11.7 percent; in 1941 it was 9.9 percent. Kendrick's TFP indexes (1929 = 100) for the two periods are as follows:[30]

Year	Index	Year	Index
1921	85.1	1941	131.3
1922	85.1	1942	133.1
1923	90.2	1943	137.3
1924	93.6	1944	147.9
1925	93.6	1945	152.9

On this crucial measure of overall productivity rise, 1941–44 comes off rather better than 1921–24, and substantially better if the terminal date is extended to 1945. The proportionate increases for the twenties are 10 percent in both periods, but 12.6 and 16.5, respectively, for the war periods 1941–44 and 1941–45. While total production declined slightly in 1945, total input fell more, especially labor input.

The American War Effort

Sustaining an approximately constant civilian labor force in the context of the enormous increase in the armed forces was a considerable feat, and an indicator that the war effort was prodigious, although in the judgment of some writers "the peak of the mobilization was still not a maximum effort."[31] The annual peak number of military personnel was 11.4 million in 1945. In ratio to the civilian labor force, this represented an increase from 1 percent in 1940 to 21 percent in the latter year. National security purchases were a huge 42 percent of GNP in the peak year 1944. The rise in the military/civilian labor force is all the more remarkable in view of the fact that the total noninstitutional population had concurrently risen by only 5 percent. The numbers in the male component of that population, black and white, were severely drained off. There were only a quarter million men between the ages of 20 and 64 who were unemployed in 1944.

On the other hand, it might be argued that if, as was widely asserted, the labor supply was the main constraint on production increase in the full-blown war economy,[32] then the woman potential was definitely not fully developed. The facts are that the number of women in the labor force increased by 5.2 million, or a third, between 1940 and 1944. By the latter year they comprised about a third of the civilian labor force. This jump brought the female participation rate (female labor force as percent of the adult female population) up from 27.9 percent to 36.3 percent. Of course, this was a historic high at that point in time. What it meant in terms of potential is a matter of judgment. That judgment may be enlightened by the fact that it was ten years later when the trend of female participation, after dropping sharply when the war ended, again reached 35 percent. But by 1970 it was 42.6 percent, and it crossed the 50 percent mark in 1978.[33] The belief that the wartime female participation rate exhausted the potential therefore seems of doubtful validity. One writer has noted that in Britain and the Soviet Union during the war only 30 percent of the women aged 14 and over were "at home," whereas in the United States about 71 percent were "at home."[34]

In any case, there were also plant and equipment capacity constraints in many lines of production by 1943, made even tighter by the widespread reluctance of business to expand capacity for fear of postwar excess capacity, which also set limits on maximum aggregate production effort.

Of course, war products might have encroached more than they did upon civilian products. What absolute encroachment there was occurred in the private investment sphere.[35] While the gross flow of investment goods contracted to a low in 1943 that was only 37 percent of the 1940 level (and much below replacement requirements), total civilian consumption, even of goods, in 1943 was higher than it had been in 1940. Even real total personal consumption expenditures per person in the civilian resident population drifted upwards during the war. This was not very severe "sacrifice," although there was additional wartime economic sacrifice with respect to work effort, commutation, and many amenities (see chapter 7).

Since the question of maximum effort largely boils down to the degree of encroachment upon civilian investment and consumption, a comparison with the more austere British civilian sacrifices can throw considerable light on that matter. In Britain, real total personal consumption at its wartime low in 1943 was 70 percent of 1938–39,[36] whereas in the United States the wartime nadir (in 1942) was about 5 percent *higher* than it had been in 1940. Alternatively viewed, personal consumption in 1943 Britain was 49 percent of NNP,[37] whereas in the United States it never fell below 55 percent of a much bigger NNP per capita.[38] This difference means that, because of the inability of Britain, in contrast to the United States, to raise its total real national income during the war,[39] the military sector had to grow at the expense of a substantial absolute drop in civilian consumption. On the labor supply side, British unemployment reduction, again in contrast to the United States, did not begin to match the required increase in its armed forces. In the United States, even while there was also some disinvestment of capital, gross private product in real terms grew 39 percent between 1940 and 1944.[40] The British effort, like the Soviet, was much closer to a maximum, and its civilian population, even with considerable American aid, a large increase in farm production, and a massive liquidation of foreign assets,[41] suffered considerable austerity and sacrifice, a self-denial that carried over into the postwar years. The U.S. civilian population, on this comparative test, did not exert a maximum war effort, although of course its relative efforts greatly exceeded those expended in World War I. John Morton Blum once wrote that the American war effort never demanded the all-out endeavor produced by other major powers because the United States entered the war late, it was far from the actual battles, and it was an incredibly abundant economy.[42]

Performance of the Economy

The previous points regarding wartime economic performance need some supplementation and elaboration. There were surely at least three outstanding economic performance achievements by the United States in World War II. The first was the elimination of unemployment. This has already been commented upon. The second was an enormous increase in the production of military goods both for the American armed forces and for the Allies. The third was holding down prices, mainly by general government controls. The two last named will be discussed in order, the first immediately following, the second in chapter 5.

The rise in constant (1947) dollar purchases of military commodities by the federal government from about $18 billion in 1941 to some $88 billion in the peak year 1944 (one-half of all commodities produced)[43] was accomplished by increasing total output and diverting considerable production from civilian products. Personal consumption and state as well as local government purchases were held down, and private investment severely curtailed. The number of new housing starts fell to 1932 depression levels.

If the military component of output is not extracted from the totals, however, then the overall economic achievement was hardly a "miracle." For example, if 1941–44 or 1941–45 be compared, again, with the peacetime cycle expansion from 1921 to 1924 or 1921 to 1925, the increases for wartime are not much better, and indeed in some important cases not as good. Wartime farm output increase was distinctly smaller for both sets of time periods. In the case of the important aggregate, real gross nonfarm product, we get the following percentage increases:[44]

1921–25	28.4%
1941–45	24.6
1921–24	26.2
1941–44	25.8

In the case of the total industrial production index (1913 = 100), however, which contains as a component much of the military output, the percentage increases are moderately reversed in the shorter of the two periods:

1921–25	52.8%
1941–45	24.7
1921–24	37.6
1941–44	44.7

Still, the differences between 1921–24 and 1941–44 are not very great. And the pattern is similar for the manufacturing output index. Perhaps the best one could say about the wartime years is that in the sphere of total industrial production almost as much was achieved in four years as the earlier peacetime cycle expansion accomplished in five. But again one must note that the terminal year 1924 was an inventory cycle recession year, which definitely weakens the thrust of the contrast.

Finally, if we look at total labor input instead of production, we find that the rise in total labor hours in all nonfarm industries in the cycle expansion of the early 1920s was distinctly greater than it was in World War II (although in the strategic manufacturing sector alone, for the 1941–44 period, labor hours rose 44.5 percent compared to

18.3 percent over 1921–24—a rise much aided by the adoption of two- and three-shift operations during the war).

If we probe beneath the aggregates, and look at particular military or military-related items, we of course find enormous increases in the output of some products. Viewing the war as a five-year period, almost 300,000 military and special-purpose aircraft were produced, 72,100 naval ships, 4,900 merchant ships, 87,000 tanks, etc.[45]

The quality of American weaponry for use in land warfare was a different matter. One historian's appraisal is that

When American forces eventually met the Germans in combat and were routed at the Battle of Kasserine Pass, it was chastening, but understandable: Green troops were fighting veterans. The humiliating and, to many people, inexcusable part was the failure of the weapons produced by American business: American tanks were not as good as German tanks; American planes were no match for German planes; American guns were outshot by German guns. With time and experience the quality of U.S. weapons would improve.[46]

But with growing combat experience, narrowing of the quality gap, and eventual overwhelming quantitative superiority, the U.S. forces gradually overcame their initial disadvantage. Besides, that disadvantage was not complete, across-the-board, for all weaponry. There was inferiority in the use of tanks, without doubt; and some disadvantage in the use of both bomber and fighter aircraft. But not so in small infantry weapons, including the standard infantry rifle.

The combined output of the war-related manufacturing, mining, and construction industries doubled between the recovery year 1939 and the peak war production year 1944.[47] To accomplish this required critical decisions, exercised in the context of an incredible lack of economic data, to divert and reallocate energy, materials, labor, and plant capacity to the needed military production centers. From one perspective, in view of the paucity of people trained in public administration, the easy way out was to rely heavily upon the decision makers in a small number of large corporations, and this was exactly what was done by the War Production Board and most of the wartime agencies.

The materials shortage was aggravated by curtailed imports. The quantity index of crude materials imports fell well below the 1940 level every year from 1942 through 1945.[48] In the cases of tin and crude rubber imports particularly, the drop was catastrophic after 1941.[49]

In cases of transport and certain strategic products the all-too-frequent instances of delay, programmatic conflicts, and outright resistance undermined the economic mobilization effort. For one thing, the normal business fear of too much excess capacity had been much aggravated by the recent prolonged depression experience. Even after U.S. entry into the war, the fear of flooded postwar markets was very common in business circles, and created a basic conflict between some industry leaders and the government. A dramatic illustration of the influence of this fear, as represented by Senator E. H. Moore of Oklahoma, occurred when Interior Secretary and Petroleum Administrator for War Harold L. Ickes testified before the Truman committee in February 1943 in behalf of the imperative need for a petroleum pipeline to be constructed from Texas to the East Coast:

Secretary Ickes. I would like to say one thing, however. I think there are certain gentlemen in the oil industry who are thinking of the competitive position after the war.

The Chairman. That is what we are afraid of, Mr. Secretary.

Secretary Ickes. That's all right. I am not doing that kind of thinking.

The Chairman. I know you are not.

Secretary Ickes. I am thinking of how best to win this war with a least possible amount of casualties and in the quickest time.

Senator Moore. Regardless, Mr. Secretary, of what the effect would be after the war? Are you not concerned with that?

Secretary Ickes. Absolutely.

Senator Moore. Are you not concerned with the economic situation with regard to existing conditions after the war?

Secretary Ickes. Terribly. But there won't be any economic situation to worry about if we don't win the war.

Senator Moore. We are going to win the war.

Secretary Ickes. We haven't won it yet.

Senator Moore. Can't we also, while we are winning the war, look beyond the war to see what the situation will be with reference to—

Secretary Ickes (interposing). That is what the automobile industry tried to do, Senator. It wouldn't convert because it was more interested in what would happen after the war. That is what the steel industry did, Senator, when it said we didn't need any more steel capacity, and we are paying the price now. If decisions are left with me, it is only fair to say that I will not take into account any post-war factor—but it can be taken out of my hands if those considerations are paid attention to.

Senator Moore. I think you will find that those of us who do look beyond the war and to the economic situation beyond the war are as much interested now in winning the war as anybody else is, but we must look to the situation developing now that may result in the unnecessary destruction—

Secretary Ickes (interposing). On that point, Senator, the Government will own this pipe line. The Government can scrap it; it can take it up; it can sell it; it can lease it; it can operate it after the war.

Senator Moore. That is what we are afraid of. We are afraid that they will not scrap it; they will not take it up but it will be sold to the people whose power it will be to destroy existing facilities, and that is what we object to.

Secretary Ickes. I am not afraid of my Government yet.

Senator Hatch. I don't think the Secretary has been quite fair to himself, because I have had many conferences with Secretary Ickes about the oil industry and about the preservation of the independent oil producer in this country, and I can say for him, which he will not say for himself, that there isn't a man in this country that is more concerned with the preservation of the independent oil men of this country than is Secretary Ickes.

Senator Moore. I am glad to hear you say that, Senator.

Senator Hatch. I so testify for you, Mr. Secretary.

Senator Moore. I say that when the bald statement is made that, "I am not concerned with anything beyond winning the war"—

Secretary Ickes. That's right; I want to win the war first.[50]

Pipelines nevertheless performed impressively in the aggregate, as table 1.1 shows; the volume increase by that type of transport was the greatest of all modes shown therein.

In addition to the vital automobile and steel industries,[51] referred to by the New Deal reformer, Secretary Ickes, railroad management and the electric power industry were other prominent examples of reluctance to expand capacity. This reluctance was shared by many who were industrial spokesmen occupying high executive positions in the war administration in Washington. In the case of electricity, it was fortunate that FDR's "socialistic" electric power projects, the great Tennessee Valley (TVA) development and the Bonneville and Grand Coulee dams, were available to fuel the crucial atomic bomb program and the vast expansion of aluminum production required for the aircraft

Table 1.1
Ton-Mile Volume of Intercity Traffic,
Public and Private,
by Kinds of Transportation, 1939–1943
(in billions of ton-miles)

Kind of Transportation	Volume 1940	Volume 1944	Percent change
Railroads	412	795	+ 93%
Motor vehicles	62	58	− 7
Inland waterways	118	150	+ 27
Oil pipelines	59	133	+125
Airways[a]	—	—	—

[a] Negligible, all years.

SOURCE: *Historical Statistics*, pt. 2, p. 707, ser. Q-12–22.

and other war industries.[52] Given this expansion of electric power, the aluminum industry did an excellent production expansion job, of course with government-financed capacity increase so large that the government owned over half the industry capacity at war's end. Some of this increased capacity went to two new entrants, Kaiser Aluminum and Chemical Corporation and Reynolds Metals Company, firms whose permanent establishment was hardly welcomed by the long-entrenched ingot monopolist, the Aluminum Company of America.

Overconfidence about capacity on the part of the steel industry, for example, on the eve of and in the early months of the war was strengthened by underestimation of the U.S. military and allied aid requirements for many materials even well after U.S. entry. Fear of peacetime excess capacity, new firm entry, and underestimation of requirements contributed to the persistence of shortages in materials in other industries throughout the entire war period.[53]

There was heated controversy over capacity expansion in the basic steel industry during the preparedness period, 1940–41. The administration itself frequently still remained publicly on the defensive about the intensity of U.S. preparations well into 1940. "I think people should realize," declared the President early in the Nazi blitzkrieg, "that we are not going to upset, any more than we have to, a great many of the normal processes of life."[54] E. A. Goldenweiser of the Federal Reserve Board told a conference of businessmen as late as September of 1940, "the emphasis at this time should be on not interfereing with the expansion of consumers' income and consumers' expenditures."[55] Various other administration spokesmen continued to play on the guns *and* butter theme, an attitude that was an expression of both neutralist influence and the New Dealers' lingering concern for overcoming the still large depression unemployment.

Official Washington and a growing number of private economic commentators reversed gears and began to sound the alarm about inadequate steel capacity in early 1941. By the second quarter of that year, expansion of the defense program and of the level of civilian demand to new high levels brought ingot capacity utilization to overfull capacity rates.[56] At this juncture the industry not only continued to advance the guns *and* butter argument, but mobilized an additional list of rationalizations that bordered much more closely on venality than on patriotism. *Iron Age* had earlier attacked a June 1940 National Resources Committee pro-expansion report by labeling its conclusions "speculative," "hypothetical," filled with estimates regarding the unpredictable, and exhibiting a sympathy for "state socialism."[57] It was contended these were only "spot shortages." The likelihood of a postwar economic collapse necessitated government tax concessions for rapid amortization of any new privately constructed plants, or better still, full public financing with private operation and the option to buy at the end of the war period. Toward the end of 1941 Bethlehem Steel alone had a billion-dollar backlog of unfilled orders.[58] *Iron Age* nevertheless still belittled the idea of a general steel shortage, and detected a New Deal plot to establish public yardstick price competition through government-owned mills.[59] The CIO's Steel Workers Organizing Committee joined the industry's resistance to expansion on the grounds that there was substantial idle capacity being held by small producers in "a score of steel ghost towns" that could be activated to employ thousands of unemployed steel workers.[60]

Basically, then, the steel makers wanted a reorientation of production from civilian to military through temporary government controls as an alternative to either private plant expansion or government ownership of new mills. The outcome of all the controversy might be described as a compromise which in a sense vindicated the industry's claims that the way to accommodate to preparedness and war was to shift from civilian to military use rather than to embark on a vast plant expansion program. In fact, wartime ingot capacity expansion was remarkably modest—only 17 percent from 1940 to 1945.[61] Nearly one-half of that increase, from 81.6 to 95.5 million short tons, was government owned.[62] And war demand was adequately provided for primarily by shifting the accompanying 19 percent production increase from civilian to war uses.

In view of the fact that raw steel production rose only 8 percent from 1941 to the 1944 wartime peak,[63] it is clear that the previous general point about the considerable diversion from civilian use in many industries indicates a fundamental aspect of the manner in which war production increases were frequently achieved, and not only in steel. The same process was also dramatically represented by crude petroleum refining capacity, the total of which rose only 12 percent between 1941 and 1945.[64] This is not to minimize the marginally strategic importance of capacity increases in steel after 1941 (for ingot capacity to 1944, about 10 percent, and for blast furnaces almost 18 percent). But recognition of the need for diversion emphasizes the vital role of wartime planning that endeavored to limit low-priority consumption and allocate the resultant short supplies.

The notorious case of synthetic rubber was rather different in that a very large increase in capacity from next to nothing was essential. The Japanese takeover of the Malay Peninsula and the Netherlands East Indies in early 1942 cut off 90 percent of the nation's supply of natural rubber, a frightening eventuality that should have been, but wasn't, anticipated in the "lost years" 1940 and 1941, when targeted construction of synthetic rubber capacity was cut down twice to a mere 10,000 tons. Years after the war Donald M. Nelson, chairman of the War Production Board, wrote, "to this day I do not understand the difficulties we encountered in building up stockpiles of rubber prior to Pearl Harbor or in erecting synthetic rubber plants."[65] In mid-1941, however, a woefully inadequate 40,000 ton facility program was recommended by William S. Knudsen, Director General of the Office of Production Management. But progress was agonizingly slow. At the beginning of 1942 the total U.S. stockpile of rubber was only 540,000 tons, about average annual peacetime consumption, and there was only one small synthetic rubber plant in existence.[66] Hence it was no exaggeration for a presidential committee under Bernard M. Baruch to report in September of that year that the stockpile depletion had created a situation so dangerous that unless corrective measures were taken at once, the country faced both military and civilian "collapse."[67] The facility construction program that was finally completed in March 1944 had a target of 877,000 long tons, financed and owned almost entirely by the federal government, and leased by the Defense Plant Corporation to private operators for $1 per year. So in the end, with the expansion of facilities and supplies of reclaimed rubber, the output of synthetic rubber jumped as follows (long tons):[68]

1941	8,383
1942	22,434
1943	231,722
1944	753,111

This was certainly a production "miracle." It must be remembered this feat required a complex decision regarding the proper chemical formulas for varied military uses, together with the appropriate raw material procurement. Furthermore, synthetic rubber production efforts became embroiled in what was at times a bitter conflict with three competing production programs that had been designated as imperative by President Roosevelt at the beginning of 1943: aircraft, high-octane aviation gasoline, and escort vessels for the merchant marine to protect cargo ships from the devastating Nazi U-boat attacks.[69]

Other achievements in the provision and production of raw materials, although not perhaps so crisis-ridden, were nonetheless impressive, e.g., in copper, brass, and, of necessity, the much disputed aviation gasoline. Later in the war even lumber became critically short. But outstandingly efficient government management resolved that crisis.[70]

These enormous increases in raw materials for war and in military matériel, and the substantial rise in GNP, were effected without any increases in the quantity of the nation's total imports over the whole period 1940–45. Moreover, while imports remained constant, the quantity of merchandise exports, practically all in the form of both military and civilian goods, more than doubled between 1940 and 1944. All this rise was concentrated in manufactured foods and finished manufactured commodities. In addition there was a large rise in the provision of transport services other than civilian motor vehicles (table 1.1).

The great bulk of the export increase was facilitated by the Lend-Lease program in aid of Britain, the USSR, and China. Britain was the chief recipient by far, and also the chief donor of "new era Lend-Lease" goods and services, mostly to the United States armed forces. Under the 1941 Lend-Lease Act, by which time Britain had almost exhausted her dollar reserves, supplies were to be provided free of charge to the recipient for the duration of the war. The recipient could *request* the supplies, and the United States would provide them *insofar as possible* within the constraints set by U.S. needs and certain provisos regarding the usages of the goods. The substantial sum of about $50 billion of Lend-Lease weapons, foodstuffs, and services was furnished through 1945, of which most were foodstuffs; and rather over $7 billion was made available in reverse Lend-Lease.[71] Britain got most and contributed most of these respective totals; and the Soviet Union received about $11 billion. The accounts with Britain were finally settled by a British payment of some $800 million.[72]

The British were bitter about some of the restraining provisos of the Lend-Lease program that the Americans believed to be reasonable. The Truman Committee expressed the severe attitude of the U.S. Congress when it declared that, "Lend-Lease was never intended as a device to shift a portion of their war costs to us, but only as a realistic recognition that they did not have the means with which to pay for materials they needed . . . assistance would be extended only where recipient was fully utilizing all of its own resources . . ."[73] One English economic historian has commented that those provisos laid down by the Congress "dominated British economic relations with the U.S.A. and the rest of the world."[74] He refers to the "onerous conditions" of what was frequently called "the most unsordid act" in history. For example, Britain was required in effect to strip herself bare of dollars and all capital assets in the United States; over two years elapsed before Lend-Lease deliveries exceeded supplies paid for in cash; sudden cancellations occurred under the act's stipulation that Lend-Lease was for the defense of the U.S.A.; and perhaps most onerous, the United States demanded that no British exports should contain any raw materials that had been supplied by Lend-Lease.[75] The United States "kindly set up an organization 'for policing observance of the terms'" of this last-named constraint. It was not until the beginning of 1945 that Britain was released from that condition. Certainly, equality of sacrifice was a principle farthest from the intent of the supporters in Congress of the Lend-Lease Act.

Chapter Two

Administration
in the Preparedness Period

THE ISOLATIONIST AND preparedness pressures within American society moved as parallel currents during the years leading up to Pearl Harbor. But as the world conflagration spread, and especially after the fall of France in June 1940, preparation for involvement on the side of the democracies surged into the ascendency. That rise to dominance is forcefully shown by the remarkable proliferation of defense planning agencies, however weak and fumbling in power and procedures, between late 1939 and December 7, 1941. Indeed, by the day "that will live in infamy" a good part of the skeletal structure, at least, of the wartime planning bureaucracy had already been set up.

The building of this preparticipation structure was facilitated politically by its piecemeal method of construction, its presentation to a strongly neutralist public in the name of defense rather than direct involvement, its support from a President who had long since been carrying on a more or less covert war with the isolationists, and its historic links with the War and Navy departments' continuing pursuit, albeit intermittent and haphazard, of their official responsibilities for planning for any future emergency. In their concern for those responsibilities the military, together with various civilian consultants like the venerable Bernard Baruch, chairman of the World War I War Industries Board, had necessarily been absorbed with applying whatever lessons were presumably to be gleaned from the rather embarrassing mobilization experiences of that war. These lessons, together with various fresh conceptions developed during the intervening two decades were imbedded in the third and "final" version of the military's Industrial Mobilization Plan (IMP) made public in the summer of 1939.

The IMP contained a recommendation for a super–planning agency (a "war resources administration"), even though it was the general belief in the administration in Washington that isolationist sentiment in Congress would reject the establishment of such an agency. The President nevertheless used his executive power to institute the War Resources Board (WRB) in August 1939. Unfortunately, the board was authorized merely to advise the long-standing, decision-making Army and Navy Munitions Board (which the President had already made responsible to himself). In fact, the WRB became essentially inoperative, even in its advisory capacity, despite the Nazi invasion of Poland on September 1 and the President's declaration of a "limited" national emergency on September 8. The WRB was additionally criticized for being probusiness and even anti–New Deal; and it ceased to function at all on November 24.

The only major emergency planning step receiving congressional blessing in that summer and fall was the passage of the Strategic Materials Act in June (see "Highlights" tabulation, chart 1.2), authorizing the acquisition and stockpiling of reserves of strategic and critical raw material imports, i.e., goods the supply of which might be cut off in wartime.

The Administration of "Control by No One"

It was not until the end of May 1940, a month of frightening Nazi advances in Western Europe following the preceding winter's "phony war," that a superagency with some recognizable functions was created to replace the defunct War Resources Board: the Advisory Commission to the old Council of National Defense (a holdover from World War I). Nor had any noteworthy subordinate planning body been created up to that time. This procrastination on the organizational front was matched by the meager increases in outlays for the army and navy through the fiscal year 1940 (see chart 1.2).

Despite the sound of its name, the Advisory Commission was designed to be the operating arm of the council in directing the defense effort, as well as an advisory body to the President. Its creation in May was a turning point in the process of building a comprehensive war planning apparatus. Under the American governmental system, as a top-level directive organization the commission had to be a presidential instrumentality, and this conformed precisely with the President's desire to spark, direct, and coordinate the defense effort himself. He engineered this centrality when he wrung from the Congress under the Reorganization Act of 1939 the authority to set up an Executive Office of the President, and at the same time received permission, in the event of a threatened or actual national emergency, to create an "office for emergency management" empowered to plan and coordinate defense mobilization.

Roosevelt brought his Office for Emergency Management (OEM) into existence on May 25, 1940, and the National Defense Advisory Commission (NDAC) was spun off from that office in the same month. The OEM and the NDAC thus deprived the War Department, as had long been the strategy of Bernard Baruch, of the formal power to direct industrial mobilization.

The NDAC was a chair-less, salary-less, almost appropriation-less apparatus for advising on coordination of the whole defense effort. Its powers resided not in formal enforcement authority but in the prestige of the Presidency and the prominent dollar-a-year men appointed to the commission, such as William S. Knudsen, president of General Motors (industrial production), and Sidney Hillman of the Amalgamated Clothing Workers (labor). Other members were presumed to be responsible, along with their staffs, for industrial materials, price stabilization, consumer protection, farm products, transportation, and somewhat later, "coordination of national defense purchases" (Donald M. Nelson of Sears, Roebuck). Later in the year other bureaus, largely ineffective, were spun off specifically to try to overcome the Armed

Services' neglect of small business in allotting military contracts, to "coordinate" defense housing, to disseminate information regarding the work of the commission to the public, and to develop contacts with the incipient state and local government defense efforts. More useful at the time and subsequently was the establishment of a badly needed Bureau of Research and Statistics under Stacy May of the Rockefeller Foundation. As the top administrative agency passed through its organizational phases into 1941 and through the war years, this strategic bureau abided, and May himself remained in charge of the War Production Board's Bureau of Planning and Statistics (following a crisis resolved in June 1943) until his resignation in September 1944.

The subdivision of the planning task in the NDAC provides an introduction to the subsequent elaborate organizational structure of top-level wartime administration. But it amounts to only an introduction, for the NDAC was a crude beginning. It was operationally weak. It reflected the nation's ambivalence about the war. Nevertheless, when its functions regarding production, procurement, and priorities were taken over in January 1941 by the newly created Office of Production Management (OPM), the NDAC and its one thousand employees could claim credit for a number of important prefatory achievements in the sphere of regulation. These included, for example, the work of the Bureau of Research and Statistics; defense labor policy guidelines; inauguration of a certification procedure for military contracts (including certification of exemption from antitrust prosecution); institution of procurement priorities and preference rating systems; the exploration of particular critical commodity scarcities; formulation of guidelines respecting government reimbursement for emergency plant facilities, depreciation, and the five-year corporate tax amortization principal on such facilities;[1] controls over profits on contracts; plus serious exploration of how to integrate the work both within a large emergency planning apparatus and between it and the military procurement services.[2] The significance of the NDAC resides not so much in its overall direction of the defense effort as in the laying of a large foundation upon which subsequent agencies could build.

But the commission was saddled with an advisory status and with nebulous authority. It had to wrestle with internal rivalries over jurisdiction and differing procedural preferences. It had to cope with War and Navy Department initiatives in military procurement. It had to push for conversion in the face of business enterprises that were inclined to give priority to current civilian demands. It was under criticism for having a business-military bias, and a big-business bias at that. And perhaps most important, it had to function without known supply capabilities or production targets. As the year of guns and butter waned, the commission itself called insistently for a substantive improvement in the loose system of economic mobilization for which it was supposed to be responsible.

The year of belated commitment to the Allied cause and stepped-up preparation for war, 1941 prior to Pearl Harbor, brought two new top-level, executive-order agencies into existence within the pro forma context of the continuing "incubator," OEM: the aforementioned OPM and later the policy-determining Supply Priorities and Allocations Board (SPAB, created in August), for which OPM was to be the operational agency. The President again refused to generate even an ostensibly operating agency with a single head to centralize the reins of authority. Instead, he created a formally impartial, tripartite policy "council" of four individuals supposed to represent management (Knudsen again), labor (Hillman again), and matériel consumers (the secretaries of War and Navy). The OPM itself was supposed to be an operating agency subordinate to the council, the "governing group," which had a dual directorship: Knudsen and Hillman.[3] These two were to forestall criticism by endowing OPM with labor-management "balance." Labor was also given recognition through the creation of a union-staffed Labor Relations Branch, as well as numerous Labor Advisory Committees on the important commodity and industry branches.[4] However, the branches paid little heed to the advice.[5] The military presence on the OPM Council was in part designed to deal with the aforementioned problems of coordination between the well-entrenched military and the executors of comprehensive plans for defense mobilization.

But the proliferation of mobilization agencies in the 1940 and 1941 defense period still left a skeletal structure that was saddled with confusion over targets, lack of enforcement power, and poor internal coordination. In spite of the vast extension of the war in Europe (including the invasion of the USSR in June 1941), the presidential declaration in May of an unlimited national emergency, the extension of the draft law, and an enormous jump in national defense purchases as 1941 unfolded, the OPM failed in many essentials almost as badly as the NDAC that its creation had demolished. While it was supposed to be the central agency responsible for the production phase of national defense, it had only the delegated power to stimulate and formulate plans for the present and the longer run, to take the lawful steps necessary, to determine the adequacy of, to expedite, to survey, analyze, and summarize requirements, to coordinate the placement of defense contracts, and to advise. It could not determine military and other related requirements, or place contracts or purchase supplies. That authority remained with the War and Navy departments, i.e., with their more or less joint Army-Navy Munitions Board, just as it had under the shadowy NDAC. Nor did the services have to go through OPM to get clearance of procurement contracts.

As Eliot Janeway points out, the whole mobilization apparatus, from NDAC through OPM and SPAB, rejected Bernard Baruch's principle of centralized command in favor of "control by no one."[6] Power over production was separated from power over prices. Power over production was also severed by the constantly feuding Armed Services and OPM. And within OPM the Priorities Division was feuding with Civilian Supply. Janeway describes Roosevelt's design of the OPM council as follows:

First there was the customer—the armed forces. Then, there was management. Finally, there was labor . . . For the war economy's customer, he provided not one but two representatives . . .

Whereas Roosevelt had appointed two spokesmen to protect one customer, the fact was that the war economy was serving two altogether distinct and often competing customers—our own armed forces and those of our Allies. The effect of limiting OPM's customer relationship to America's armed forces was to pervert the principle of civilian control over production . . . When its harassed and bewildered officials demanded that production be geared to military strategy, their customer—the Army and Navy—told them to mind their own business . . . [7]

The execution of priority orders for delivery of goods to the army and navy, to the emerging foreign friends (including Lend-Lease, which was at presidential discretion), to the subcontractors of prime contractors, and to civilian purchasers was no more subject to quantitative controls, to say nothing of integrated planning, than it had been with the NDAC, until belated presidential action in August wrought slight improvement. The lines of authority within OPM were often distressingly unclear. Furthermore, the services themselves were confused about the time factor and were not setting firm targets for either capacity expansion or the immediate fulfillment of matériel and human requirements—a lack for which they could not very well be blamed during the preparatory period. Also, the rudimentary organization of OPM's all-important commodity sections delayed any rationally disaggregated flow of goods until well into the fall of the year. OPM had to accept the requirements for goods as stipulated by the services, and could only then translate these into priorities—a procedure which left the affected parts of the civilian sector (including the parts judged essential) increasingly encroached upon yet lacking power of correction.

This disjointed state of affairs could be easily endured in the slack economy of 1940, but in the late months of 1941 it became ever more intolerable. Cases in point during the latter period were materials such as aluminum, copper, steel, and natural rubber; consumer-related capital equipment such as machine tools; and consumer durable products containing critical components, such as automobiles. As can be inferred from this illustration, it was most unfortunate that the mobilization planning task did not have access to the later pioneering work of W. W. Leontief, who developed a comprehensive matrix showing the input-output flows for all the major sectors of the economy.

A Leontief matrix would have helped, but it probably would not have made a substantive difference. The approach resorted to before, but especially during, the war was in many respects very similar to the British wartime administration as described by Joan Mitchell. Requirements and priorities in the United Kingdom were:

whatever supply would be acceptable enough that neither officials, nor at a later stage, Ministers would feel justified in making a political issue of it. Neither market demands nor consumers' preferences came into it. Since budgets were prepared for a limited number of specific and relatively homogeneous commodities (notably steel, coal, timber, some non-ferrous metals, some chemicals) the calculations could be done in physical quantities.

Since there was no question of maximizing the total product, but only the military part of it, and that in certain specific forms, the budgets never needed summing to fit into a total input-output scheme, and a standard of valuation was not necessary.[8]

Reconciliation of the various requirements, priorities, and preference orders, in the United States as in Britain, was done by trial and error, successive approximations, and the use of clout.

The above-mentioned presidential administrative action in August 1941 was the creation of SPAB, which was followed in a month by a reorganization of OPM. These moves clearly attested to the experimental nature of, and the operational defects in, the new planning machinery. SPAB was another superagency on top of OPM, one that replaced the former OPM overall policy council. Under this new arrangement the operating agencies of defense mobilization were the OPM, the Armed Services, and the Office of Price Administration (OPA). Civilian Supply was a division of OPM. At the same time, there was some attempt to expand and administratively tighten up the vital commodity sections of OPM, but renaming them industry and commodity "branches" revealed a sore lack of the needed thrust. What was desperately called for was correction of intraorganizational fragmentation and the duplication among the commodity sections.

That the defense effort in the spheres of facilities and matériel production was actually moving ahead in many, though not all, sectors in the face of an ungainly, lumbering, tortuously fashioned administrative structure is to be explained largely as an ordinary responsiveness of industry to increased (frequently uncoordinated as between army and navy) orders from the Armed Services and from Lend-Lease, orders lustily backed up by an explosion of federal funding. Basically, market forces were still in operation. In the case of farm products, the historical fear of surpluses and reticence about postwar prospects required Agriculture Department initiatives belatedly calling for stepped-up production (the "Food for Freedom" drive) during the fall of 1941.[9]

The unfolding pattern of administration affecting the industrial sector was exactly what would be expected of a society based upon, and ideologically oriented toward, the private, administered-market economy. To build a public planning superstructure and to coordinate planning with execution in such a milieu required a new and strange expertise, an expertise that could not readily be conceptualized by corporate executives whose background was foreign to comprehensive social planning. Public administration has to subordinate and translate the familiar micro-level pecuniary calculus to a macro-level engineering framework. Public administration requires criteria quite different from private business criteria, and the lacuna has only recently begun to be closed with the use of cost-benefit analysis. One of the classic studies of World War II planning comments on this problem with particular reference to the absence of appropriate measures of mobilization performance:

Private business has its dollar accounting, yielding quantitative, additive, and comparable measures of profit and loss. But most applications of government policy do not make a specific record of achievement in common units of measure. There is no evidence of the appropriateness of a particular administrative procedure which carries the conviction of positive achievement in dollars and cents. No standard has been developed as an alternative to dollar profits. There is no yardstick of demonstrable proof other than logic and the voice of the individual proponent of a particular practice in a specific situation.[10]

Thus there were great obstacles to administrative mobilization, and these were all the more formidable by virtue of the widespread, corroding ambivalence about an all-out effort. The nation was not yet at war. After Pearl Harbor, while wartime direction of the economy was no bed of roses, the barriers were breached. Meanwhile,

At every step, decisions to institute controls had to contend with the opposition of those who disbelieved in the urgency of the growing crisis, the natural preference of large segments of industry for free market conditions and their resentment of control from the top, the absence of a program of military requirements scheduled forward to cover the inevitable expansion of needs, and the overwhelming tendency to act as if the emergency would be of short duration.[11]

Such was 1941. The creation of SPAB did help the planning machinery to inch forward. The reorganization package properly endowed the civilian supply sector with more recognition. It effected a partial reconciliation of the disparate policies impinging upon that sector as they were inherited from the NDAC and OPM's pre-SPAB period.

The earliest arrangement had functioned with a Price Stabilization Division under economist Leon Henderson that was separate from the "Consumer Protection" division under Harriett Elliott, political scientist from the University of North Carolina. The intent in April 1941 was to correct this uncomfortable detachment through the formation of the Office of Price Administration and Civilian Supply (OPACS)— under Henderson. While this provided, after a fashion, a continuing agency for pursuing the legally unenforceable, and hence thankless, price control task (wholesale prices rose 13 percent between March and September 1941), it left essentially unsolved the problem of administering the supply of civilian essential and nonessential products.

OPACS was supposed to be responsible for the distribution of residual civilian products remaining after the provision of defense needs. That prior allocative decision was already in April definitively delegated to the Priorities Division of OPM. OPACS was only to *guide* OPM in this matter; OPM was to continue to issue priority orders that would hopefully be integrable with OPACS' residual scheduling!

This was the definitive ruling projected by John Lord O'Brian, General Counsel of OPM, on April 23, 1941, and OPM subsequently administered priorities in accordance with it.[12] The entirely legitimate conflict over the initiative on priorities between OPM and OPACS became more heated in May and June. Henderson was disturbed over the continued high level of automobile production, and also feared many civilian industries and small businesses might have to cut output and employment because they could not get materials. But O'Brian stood firm, supporting his stand in part by the argument that since military and civilian needs could not be separated for priorities purposes, *one* agency should have exclusive administration.[13] OPACS retorted that the concept of *essential* civilian use was clear and not dependent upon the classification defense/nondefense. And so the tussle continued, with OPM's Division of Priorities making the basic decisions, even as the two contestants made a vain effort to work together and their conflict approached an open break. But there was no integrated planning of priorities, especially as the matter impinged upon curtailment of civilian supplies. It was ironic that OPM itself was de facto subordinate to the Armed Services in the priorities game, and was unable to move effectively toward a solution of the civilian supply problem.[14]

The creation of SPAB on August 28 was offered as a solution, but as a Bureau of the Budget analyst was subsequently to comment, SPAB simply transformed "the problem of coordinating OPM and OPACS from an interagency problem to an intra-agency matter."[15] As we shall see below, civilian supply continued to be a poor relation when SPAB was transformed into the War Production Board. The problem was more than an intra-agency matter, for the War and Navy departments held the trump curtailment cards. Both ends of the acronym were defective: price control was ineffective and civilian supplies could not be assessed by the OPACS-SPAB combination.[16]

The failure to build a tight-knit planning and operating machinery continued after August when OPACS was appropriately terminated and replaced by the Office of Price Administration, the enduring wartime agency of price control and rationing. In September the civilian supply function was assigned to a division of OPM (under Henderson), with SPAB, of course, granted ultimate formal authority of broad policy determination. This resolution was probably as sensible as any that could be contrived under the circumstances, for by this time the allocative conflict between the military, the foreign, and the two divisions of the civilian was becoming acute; it was no longer merely a matter of particular scarcities.

The Mobilization of Labor

The cooperation, mobilization, and integration of civilian labor into the defense and subsequently the war effort required a four-pronged program: recruitment/placement, training, wage and hour stabilization, and labor-management détente. During the period of defense preparation under the NDAC and OPM, with so many millions still unemployed, the training task was programatically given preference over recruitment and placement in the slowly accelerating defense work. This part of the government's programs was more successfully organized than was the planning apparatus in the area of nonhuman production inputs, where the mobilization problems were more acute.[17] Under the direction of Sidney Hillman's Employment Division (later "Labor Division") of the NDAC, an impressive vocational training endeavor was instituted. Reliance was placed upon both training within industry and the existing network of schools and colleges. The New Deal's Civilian Conservation Corps, Works Progress Administration, and National Youth Administration were all adapted and harnessed to the vocational and engineering education task. By January 31, 1942, over 600,000 trainees were currently involved, and the cumulative total was 3.3 million in the various component programs.[18] The Training-Within-Industry program was almost equally as large, and was continued under the War Manpower Commission (WMC) during the war.[19]

As for recruitment and placement, the OPM period spanning most of 1941 brought the Labor Division of NDAC and most of its staff into OPM in March, again with Sidney Hillman, as both associate director of OPM and director of its Labor Division. The latter operated throughout that year of adequate overall labor supply. But placement in the expanding defense activities, involving some transfers away from priority-created unemployment and slowed employment in some civilian industries, became a more vital task than it had been in 1940. The attempt to handle these pressures, together with a considerable expansion of the training program, prompted breaking the OPM Labor Division into two sections. One was concerned with labor supply and priorities, and properly developed a close liaison with the well-established U.S. Employment Service, which throughout the war was the most important civilian agency concerned with labor supply.[20] The other was responsible for the defense training effort. Working closely with the two, but independently administered, was the Training-Within-Industry Branch.[21]

By the time of Pearl Harbor the accomplishments of the Labor Division's training program had been so impressive that it should easily have been awarded the prize among all defense mobilization agencies, had one been offered, for operational efficiency. The division had been remarkably successful in enlisting the cooperation of labor, government, private institutions, and employers regarding the utilization of existing vocational education facilities (a new facilities construction program was unnecessary), and in the adaptation of public employment programs to defense training purposes. While the onset and conduct of the war itself brought small recruitment and placement crises, there was never any general training crisis.

The need to control the competitive bidding up of wages by defense employers to get workers, from other defense industries if necessary, first emerged critically through the spread of the practice in both Pacific and Atlantic Coast shipyards in mid-1940.[22] The first major step by the NDAC in the matter was the appointment of a broad Shipbuilding Stabilization Committee in late November 1940. However, comparative peace in the shipyards induced general inaction until after the Labor Division was transferred to the OPM in March 1941. By this time the labor markets were getting tighter, particularly in the shipyards. Critical issues to be dealt with included skilled rates of pay, shift premiums, overtime provisions, strikes/lockouts, agreements not to limit production, grievance machinery, and arbitration procedures.[23] A tentative, two-year agreement between Pacific Coast labor and employers was reached in April 1941. Differences were to be referred to the Labor Department's Conciliation Service, and if necessary, resolved by arbitration. The OPM Labor Division was an active participant, as it was in subsequent months, in similar settlements affecting the Great Lakes, the Atlantic Coast, and the Gulf. The agreements did not by any means bring peace, and the OPM was kept extremely busy mediating disputes throughout 1941. On top of that caseload, Hillman's office after Pearl Harbor had to monitor the the labor implications of a December 10 presidential demand that all matériel plants would have to go on a 168-hour week.[24] In many cases there were not enough workers to operate these shifts, and the new requirement raised difficulties over the resultant absenteeism and overtime implications, all of which added to the Labor Division's burden. Additionally, stabilization work had to be done in other industries, such as aircraft and the building trades; and the upsurge of strikes in 1941 greatly increased the stabilization and negotiation responsibilities of both the Labor Division of OPM and the National Defense Mediation Board. "Hillman was still calling for stabilization and the establishment of ceilings . . . with wages equalized, in February 1942, and nothing effective was done . . . until the beginning of 1943."[25]

Clearly the general problems of labor-management relations during the period of preparation became increasingly difficult. Labor, and particularly organized labor, was by no means wedded to the idea of national unity above all; or to surrendering job rights, such as seniority, when transferring from nondefense to defense work.[26] It certainly was not yet prepared to render the no-strike pledge to which it committed itself later in the year after Pearl Harbor. Its response in this respect to the President's May 1941 unlimited national emergency declaration was lukewarm. Indeed, whereas the recovery year 1940, of stable consumer prices and large unemployment, witnessed 2,500 strikes with 6.7 million labor-days idle, the year 1941 produced 4,300 strikes with 23.1 million labor-days idle, most of which was pyramided into the year's first half. In 1941, unemployment was dropping, employment and living costs were rising, expanding defense industries were opening expectations for competitive organizing drives by different unions; wage rates in some sectors were lagging behind both sporadic wage increases (e.g., in steel) and prices; and profits were mounting.[27] Also, isolationist and neutralist sentiments still operated to undermine the patriotic impulse.

The consequent restiveness of labor was aggravated by the apprehension of the current portentous shift of economic and political power from labor to business inaugurated by the new defense mobilization agencies. To many in labor's ranks and elsewhere the leadership of those agencies appeared to symbolize and foreshadow the scuttling of the New Deal political coalition and its liberal policies. The New Deal prolabor setting had already begun to deteriorate even before the defense upsurge. Several states, for example, had passed legislation in 1939 imposing constraints on unions similar to those applying to employers under the Wagner Act—an anticipation of the Taft-Hartley Act and the state "right-to-work" laws of 1947. But it was defense, and later war, administration that almost of necessity induced a reversal of the depression's dethronement of big business. Of course, the President blundered inexplicably when he created a War Resources Board in August 1939 with Edward Stettinius of U.S. Steel at its head, and containing no representatives from labor (or agriculture). When the board was replaced by the NDAC, the formal requirements of a broadly oriented agency leadership were met, and this policy was to be for the duration. But meeting the formal requisites still meant a de facto re-enthronement of business, and given the concentrated structure of American manufacturing, it could not be small business.

Industrial relations in the NDAC period, with Hillman at the agency's helm for labor starting in October 1940, were endowed with a certain euphoria by virtue of the aforementioned quiet recovery phase of the economic cycle, the acceptance of collective bargaining by some of the greatest industries,[28] and the satisfactions attending substantial advances in union membership. However, quite a furor on the part of labor's opponents was caused when the Advisory Commission issued labor policy statements on August 31 and September 6 declaring in part that "All work carried on as part of the defense program should comply with . . . the Walsh-Healey Act, Fair Labor Standards Act, the National Labor Relations Act, etc . . . " WPB historian Richard Purcell notes, "This was at a time when such indispensable defense manufacturers as the Bethlehem Steel Corporation, Ford Motor Company, General Motors Corporation, Todd Shipbuilding Company, were under charges of the National Labor Relations Board."[29] Should vital defense production be estopped pending the outcome of such disputes? The War and Navy departments expressed nominal agreement with the commission's labor policy, but they were not bound by it in practice.[30] Many in the union ranks in late 1940 were insistent that application of the NDAC labor policy meant no defense contracts should go to violators of the labor laws. Some unions condemned Hillman for condoning awards of such contracts.[31] Controversy regarding defense contracts policy persisted after the establishment of the OPM. But in fact, "neither OPM nor its successor, the War Production Board, used the priority authority or the power to let contracts for the purpose of enforcing social policy."[32]

The big employers' organizations meanwhile were becoming increasingly vocal against alleged union power, what they thought was the bias of the labor laws, and the infiltration of the unions by communists. Furthermore, as the economy moved toward tighter labor markets in late 1940 and in 1941, the pressure for more clout to ensure uninterrupted production and wage stabilization rose in keeping with labor's concomitant activism. Both sides of the labor-management antagonism were using the mobilization to further their own economic and political aims. Bills were introduced into both houses of Congress that would require the compulsory settlement of industrial disputes. Wartime was indeed the seedtime of the Taft-Hartley law. The administrative upshot of all the turmoil was the creation on March 19, 1941, by Executive Order, of the National Defense Mediation Board (NDMB), a tripartite (labor, management, the public) body of eleven men that significantly enough supplanted the New Deal's National Labor Relations Board. AFL resentment in particular against CIO Hillman and his Labor Division of the NDAC was assuaged by the appointment of two AFL officials among the four labor members of the board.

Meanwhile, in June, the growth of defense employment, black militancy, and the encouragement afforded by the CIO's nondiscriminatory membership policy conjoined to force the President to establish the Fair Employment Practices Committee within the OPM. The OPM prominority effort was vigorous and reasonably successful.[33] The FEPC endured through subsequent agency reorganizations until Congress let it lapse during the 1946 demobilization.

The NDMB had no enforcement powers and could only handle cases certified to it by the Secretary of Labor after the mediation efforts of the Labor Department's Conciliation Service had failed. It remained the exclusive defense-period industrial relations agency until November, when its rejection of the United Mine Workers' demand for a union shop in the captive mines of the steel industry (mines used exclusively by their producer in an integrated operation) prompted the resignation of the CIO representatives.

But much of the 1941 turbulence in labor-management relations bypassed the mediation process. Less than a fortnight after the May declaration of national emergency the army took over the strikebound plant of the North American Aviation Co. in Los Angeles. Concomitantly, the director of Selective Service canceled essential-work draft deferments whenever an employee in a dispute ceased to work at his or her job. But even as government and the public more and more took a tougher stance toward industrial disputes, the increasing awareness of imminent involvement in the war reduced the heat of such conflicts and prepared labor for the wartime no-strike pledge.

Agriculture and Food

In one vitally important area of the economy it was not necessary to erect a big new administrative structure, either during the defense mobilization or later during the war itself. That was agriculture. The reason is readily apparent: the New Deal had built through the Department of Agriculture an elaborate public management apparatus on top of the long-established, far-flung network of land grant college agricultural schools, Experiment Stations, and the Agricultural Extension Services of the land grant colleges with their myriad county agents, together with ample research facilities including the department's prestigious Bureau of Agricultural Economics. The farm sector therefore already possessed its federal planning and directive agency responsible for output and price planning of major products, soil conservation, subsidization, crop storage, marketing, and technological improvement.

Nevertheless, the process of changing the production signals from restriction to expansion was not simple or easy. There was, for example, the necessity of dealing with the attitude similar to industry's that war's end might leave producers with excess capacity, an attitude superimposed upon farmers' chronic fear of surpluses. Also, while the existence of very articulate private farm organizations was in one sense a planning advantage, the rival objectives between the groups, with each one maximizing, according to its own viewpoint, the position of its constituency, often made for conflicts that undermined the fashioning of effective national policies. For example, the National Farmers Union during the war consistently advocated subsidies instead of raising farm price ceilings, in order to hold down increases in living costs—and won its point when in April 1943 subsidies were extended by the government in order to "hold the line" on the entire wage-price system.[35] Both the Farm Bureau and the National Grange pushed for the removal of subsidies and for other policies that could well have undermined effective price control by OPACS and OPA. The farm organizations frequently clashed with the department, as was the case, for example, with regard to the levels at which commodity loan rates should be set. [36]

While the Agriculture Department retained its position as the central planning organization for farming within the wartime administrative hierarchy, it of course could not escape the policy and administrative difficulties stemming from the fact that the other agencies exercised decision-making authority over the vital nonfarm activities that were economically interconnected with the agricultural sector. For example, after the war's onset the WPB was given control over supplies required for both farm production and food processing. It was not until December 1942 that the authority of the Food Requirements Committee of the WPB to oversee food production and allocation was transferred to the Agriculture Department. However, the department possessed only a veto power over price ceilings.

At that same time, two primary food control agencies were created within the department: the Food Production Administration and the Food Distribution Administration. It was these two that in the spring of 1943 were fused into a single War Food Administration (WFA), albeit under a newly appointed administrator, Chester Davis, not Secretary Charles Wickard. [37] In effect, the Secretary's responsibilities were relegated to nonwar, residual activities of the department.

Henceforth, the WFA, within the department, was the primary coordinator of the whole food program, including the very large-scale purchasing of food for Lend-Lease. But even at that late juncture in the war, its coordination work was sorely beset with restraints on its freedom of action, restraints exercised by both the Congress and the other war agencies. It was the chronic dilemma of U.S. wartime planning, and indeed of economic planning under any circumstances: separate agencies responsible for directing nonseparable parts of a system. The cross-currents are well summarized by Walter Wilcox:

The Office of Price Administration administered the controls over prices provided by the Emergency Price Control Act. Selective Service, the War Manpower Commission, and the War Labor Board administered the wartime controls over manpower and wages. The Office of Defense Transportation exercised the President's war powers in the field of inland transportation. In the international field, the Board of Economic Warfare and its successor, the Foreign Economic Administration, exercised the wartime functions of granting export and import licenses on food and agricultural products, purchasing supplies and undertaking programs to stimulate food production in foreign countries. Ocean shipping was coordinated and controlled by still another war agency, the War Shipping Administration.[38]

While Wilcox is referring to the pre-WFA period, the problems of interagency disjunction persisted throughout the remainder of the war. But the managers in the planning-operating bureaucracy did in their improvising way lead toward ultimate victory: most of the time their administrative mistakes and internecine conflicts over how to do the job were subordinated to agreement regarding how to get on with the job.

Chapter Three

Two Studies
in Wartime Business:
Farming and Small Enterprise

AMERICAN FARMING FOUND itself, as U.S. involvement approached, wrestling with the long-standing problems of excess capacity, disguised unemployment, marginal entrepreneurs, and product surpluses.[1] Its productivity record in the quarter-century before 1941 had been mediocre. Defense Commissioner for Agriculture Chester Davis proposed in November 1940 that 5,000,000 low-income farm people leave agriculture and prepare to find employment in defense industries, adding, "we have an abundance of food and fiber to meet normal civilian requirements and any military demand that may arise. On top of that, the surpluses are piling up which would have gone into export had there been no war in Europe . . . ."[2] There was the familiar fear that capacity expansion for defense and possible war would aggravate the twin postwar threats of overextension (as in World War I) and a massive return to farming by demobilized military personnel. Inventories were large, equal to almost two years' supply in the case of certain major crops.

Yet by the fall of 1942 there were already domestic shortages, for example, of meat, fats, oils, dairy products, and canned foods, shortages exacerbated by the cutting off of Pacific sources of sugar, oil, fruit, and other foodstuffs[3] and by the enormous requirements of Allied countries. While the total quantity of imports of crude and manufactured foods fluctuated rather narrowly from 1940 through 1945, and exports of crude foods were also fairly stable from 1940 through 1944, exports of manufactured foods increased manyfold, due mostly to aid to the Allies and supplying U.S. armed forces abroad.

Farm production was initially increased in response to the wartime stimulus. But the increase was by far the greatest in livestock and related products, as the following production indexes show (1967 = 100):

	Livestock and products	Crops	Total farm output
1940	60	66	60
1941	64	68	62
1942	71	76	69
1943	77	71	68
1944	73	75	70
1945	73	73	69

It will be seen that the substantial livestock production increases continued through 1943, whereas in the case of crops the increases stopped a year earlier, and the decrease in 1943, partly because of scattered droughts and floods, was barely recouped. The quite moderate increases in total production were still sufficient to actually enlarge in most cases, with the notable exception of corn, the already huge stocks existing on the eve of U.S. entry into the war.

The augmented total production was accompanied on the input side by an even more modest rise in total land in farms. However, there was a dramatic shift from cropland to pastureland. The latter increased by 22 percent between 1940 and 1945, exactly as much as the output of livestock and products. But output *per acre of cropland* exhibited a much better productivity performance, for the crop production rise was effected with a 15 percent drop in farm cropland and only a 4 percent rise in 1945 crop acreage harvested as compared with 1940. Since the total inputs of labor hours in all crop production (but not in livestock) declined slightly over the whole period, we have to look at other inputs to explain the rise in crop production. And indeed, inputs of two important items did rise notably: fertilizer and liming materials; and mechanical power (including electricity) and machinery.[4] Unlike the nonfarm civilian industrial sector, the farm sector was certainly in general, except for the one year 1943, not starved for fixed reproducible capital goods (other than for buildings). The mechanical power and machinery index rose by a third between 1940 and 1945. Walter Wilcox concludes that

taking the war period as a whole, farmers made substantial additions to their equipment . . . there was a net gain of 75,000 tractors in 1942 and 34,000 more in 1943. Sales of almost every category of farm equipment for use in the United States were higher in 1944–45 than in 1939–40 . . .

Losses resulting from inability to harvest the crop . . . were at a minimum throughout the war period. The farm machinery program, which directed the use of the limited quantities of steel available first into repair parts and second into machines most urgently needed to help in meeting the annual goals, together with rationing, played an important part in getting the increased acreages of the different crops grown and harvested.[5]

The tractor and farm machinery program for wartime was nevertheless the subject of much dispute all during the period preceding the discontinuance of farm machinery rationing in November 1944. In this case the Truman Committee's influence was telling. Production of farm machinery was severely restrained during 1942 and 1943, 80 percent and only 40 percent, respectively, of the comparatively high 1940 level. But in 1944 the increased production of tractors for farm use, following a partial victory for the profarm advocates, was 85 percent of 1940.[6] While the average for 1942 and 1943, relative to 1940, was not much below the relative levels for producers durable equipment in the economy generally, it was argued cogently by the Department of Agriculture, the Farm Machinery and Equipment Branch of the War Production Board, and the Truman Committee that the reduced complement of farm crop labor required a substantial increase in the capital/labor ratio if productivity and production were to rise to meet wartime needs.[7] These proponents encountered opposition not only from the WPB and its Office of Civilian Supply but even from the Smaller War Plants Corporation, which in this case was somewhat overenthused in its commitment to concentrate production in the hands of the smaller of the 1,600 firms manufacturing farm machinery and parts.[8] As it turned out, and as the above indexes for farm crop and total output might suggest, there was a drop in total factor productivity in agriculture, after the initial rise through 1942, that lasted for the remainder of the war.[9]

Meanwhile, the market value of farm production soared as farm prices jumped upward, especially between 1940 and 1943. The price indexes for the period are as follows (1967 = 100):

	Prices received	Prices paid	Percent of "parity"
1940	39	36	81
1941	49	39	93
1942	63	44	105
1943	76	50	113
1944	78	53	108
1945	81	56	109

After years of relative price disadvantage, the price-conscious farmer was experiencing a somewhat compensatory second "golden age."[10] The farmer's share of a typical market basket of farm food products jumped from 40 percent in 1940 to 53 percent in 1945. There was a particularly rapid rise in the low average farm income per farm operator as compared to nonfarm business and professional incomes.[11] While the number of farms declined only 4 percent, the number of mortgaged farms fell 27 percent, the total value of farm real estate jumped 79 percent, and the total of outstanding farm real estate indebtedness decreased from $6.6 billion in 1939 to $4.8 billion in 1945.[12]

Moderate structural and related changes were taking place in the farm sector, most of which were a continuation of long trends. There was, for example, an absolute decline of 3,000 in the number of farms. But this fall was similar to that for 1935–40 and 1945–50, all of which were moderate declines compared with the large decreases in the period 1950–70. Wartime prosperity operated to arrest the more rapid long term downward trend that set in soon after the war.[13] The net out-migration of *people* from farms exceeded 6 million between 1940 and the end of 1945, even though agricultural *employment* fell by only a million. The decline in the South's farm population, especially among blacks, was particularly large.[14] And there was no postwar returning (except for brief influx ripples in 1945 and 1947).

Farms grew larger in size, a continuation of the long-run movement. Average acreage per farm, for example, had been 175 in 1940, but five years later it was up to 195, about the same rate of increase as had occurred in the preceding five years. While the number of fully or partly owned farms increased by over a quarter-million, the number of tenant farms decreased by over half a million, another testimony to both the favorable economic conditions for agriculture that obtained during the war and to the lure, especially for blacks, of wartime non-farm jobs. The number of farm cooperatives drifted slowly downward, pretty much on trend.

The proportion of farm personal income from nonfarm sources to income from farm sources declined notably during the war, and this was contrary to the long-run pattern. Again, the wartime increase in reliance upon income from farm sources no doubt reflected prosperity on the farm. If there was a "miracle" in total food and fiber production, it was due primarily to market and government demand stimuli and only secondarily to superior administrative organization by federal war agencies. This is in contrast with the British experience, where deliberate, locally administered government planning and direction did perform a production miracle. It raised the amount of cultivated arable land by 50 percent and additionally raised per acre crop yields substantially by changes in production techniques similar to the American pattern.[15]

Nonfarm Business

The war brought prosperity, on the whole, to those nonfarm firms that continued in operation. Many marginal smaller firms went out of business, however. The slow rise in the total number of enterprises, a return to the long-run trend that had begun after the depression nadir in 1933, was reversed; and 324,000 nonfarm concerns exited from the total between 1940 and 1945. That was a significant 10 percent of the 1940 total.[16] Both corporations and unincorporated firms were heavily represented in the mortality record as revealed in the very rough estimates of business numbers, and the proportionate declines were about the same. Significant decreases occurred in construction, retail trade, and service activities, all havens of small enterprise. But there was, of course, an increase in the number of firms in manufacturing, as expansion in wartime demand for such products through 1942 boosted sales and income. Then the number grew slowly through the remaining war years.

A significant indicator of business conditions is the failure rate — the number of failures per 10,000 listed concerns. According to Dun and Bradstreet's record, this rate declined sharply and steadily from 1940 through 1945, just as it had during World War I, and its level during World War II was far below that for the "prosperous" 1920s.[17] A second major indicator is business income, and here again the overall picture for business under wartime constraints is favorable. Corporate profit before and after income and excess profits taxes, and the profit rate, in billions of dollars and percent, was:[18]

	Before taxes	After taxes	After tax/ before tax	After tax/ total assets
1940	9.5	6.9	72.6%	2.2%
1941	16.6	9.5	57.2	2.8
1942	23.3	11.1	47.6	3.1
1943	28.0	12.2	43.6	3.1
1944	26.5	11.7	44.2	2.8
1945	21.2	10.5	49.5	2.4
1948	34.2	22.5	65.8	4.3

It seems clear that profitability after taxes was constrained during the war years. But given the almost riskless, high-level aggregate economic setting, the corporate pecuniary sacrifice was modest. Of course, the profitability record compared very favorably with the preceding depression years. Aside from an increased tax take, business as a whole, *for those remaining active*, fared quite well. The year 1948, a quite successful postwar year, is inserted into the tabulation for comparison.

Protecting Small Business: Administrative Failure

The manufacturing sector became a battleground, as small enterprise in that sector fought to retain a place for itself, especially in the matter of its share of military orders and of materials and manpower for the production of scarce civilian products. In the early stages of defense and war procurement small manufacturers were widely ignored,[19] despite the background of the bills passed by Congress to aid small business between 1933 and 1942. The procurement agencies of the army and the navy favored the larger concern on grounds of timing and efficiency,[20] and they may well have been correct. In the arena of "essential" civilian supply, the smaller manufacturer suffered severe shortage of materials, partly because of disagreements between such people as Leon Henderson, Office of Price Administration, and William S. Knudsen, Office of Production Management, over what constituted essential civilian needs.[21] Administrative difficulties were further compounded by hoarding of materials by larger manufacturers, especially in 1941 and 1942.[22]

Donald M. Nelson, at that time a member of the staff of the Advisory Commission to the Council of National Defense, was assigned to develop both a prime contract and a subcontract program for small enterprise later in 1940. But the army, the navy, and most large prime contractors were hostile to the idea. These groups believed at the time and throughout the war that it was easier and faster to buy from the middle and larger firms, which they believed were most likely to produce good quality products at "reasonable" prices. Such belief probably reflected the normal functioning of a concentrated enterprise system. They retained this viewpoint throughout the entire post–World War II defense procurement era, i.e., long after an emergency justification for it had passed.

Nelson's initial program hardly got off the ground. The generalization applies equally to the "program" following an administrative shift to the Bureau of Defense Contract Service of the OPM in July 1941. Nelson himself commented that the subsequently established War Production Board, of which Nelson was made chairman, merely "surveyed" the small enterprise war orders problem "well into 1942."[23]

The government's intent from the beginning was to utilize available small enterprise facilities, ensure equity in procurement, and protect the small business sector during the emergency so that when peace came the oligopolistic business sector would not have augmented its market power vis-à-vis the small enterprise sector of the industrial economy. The need for such an orientation was underscored by the wartime suspension of antitrust activity.

Unfortunately, poor results of the government's early efforts led to another administrative shift in September 1941. At that time the program was shunted to the Division of Contract Distribution of the OPM, with investment banker Floyd B. Odlum as director. This was another "determined move," the program lacking authority to do anything, but with an incipient bureaucracy of forty to fifty people in Washington, thirty-nine field offices, and a field staff of about four hundred employees. Later expansion raised this to twelve hundred employees and one hundred field offices.[24] Actually, Odlum's policy favored deflection from a policy of getting war contracts for small business, for he, like his second successor in the subsequent Smaller War Plants Corporation, Brigadier General Robert Johnson, preferred rather to help small manufacturers produce for essential *civilian* needs.[25] The major small business complaints, in addition to the aforementioned hoarding by the larger manufacturers, included inability to make cost estimates in a form satisfactory to the military procurement officers, inability to procure even nonhoarded materials, and lack of even elementary information on procurement opportunities. It was about this time that the harsh quip became prevalent: a small firm was "any business that is unable to maintain a staff in Washington to represent its interest."[26] The numerous field offices were presumed to help overcome this drawback.

By the time of the next administrative shift in January 1942, when the OPM was absorbed by the WPB, the "Division of Contract Distribution" estimated that 10,000 of the "larger smaller plants" had war contracts, but 140,000 did not. A Senate committee observed that the division "was an advisory agent to an advisory agent to procurement divisions which were independent and showed little willingness to accept advice."[27]

Meanwhile, the time-hallowed Senate and House committees on small business continued to function largely as lightning rods for the flood of small enterprise complaints. The Senate committee, in a February 1942 report, noted that 56 of the country's estimated 184,000 manufacturing *establishments* (*Historical Statistics* lists 230,000 *firms* in 1941) had been awarded 75 percent of Army and Navy contracts.[28]

In view of the patent failure on the small business front, Congress was impelled to establish, with presidential approval, on June 11, 1942, the Smaller War Plants Corporation (SWPC)[29] to lend to small enterprises and otherwise aid them in the procurement scramble. The small business program became centered in that agency. Its deputy chairman and board of directors were to be appointed by and responsible to the chairman of the WPB. But the executive order authorizing action was not issued until September 8!

That was not all. Nelson subsequently wrote of the new SWPC that "its going was not made easier by the institution of the Controlled Materials Plan"[30] (CMP). The chief reason for this gloomy appraisal was that the undoubtedly efficient CMP program for integrated allocation of materials, gradually made effective over the period from its belated establishment in November 1942 to mid-1943, shifted the administration of materials allocation from the civilian-dominated WPB to the military services and the Maritime Commission (responsible, together with the emergency War Shipping Adminstration, for the merchant marine program). This meant that the secondary power of materials allocation was in effect delegated to private, large prime contractors who then had the authority to pass the allocations on down through the rest of the industrial system.[31] Hence Nelson commented that, although CMP had to be adopted, it increased the semifeudal dependence of small business upon big and middle-sized business.[32]

CMP therefore brought into 1943, the year of peak war production, the solidification of the continued dominance of the military in the procurement process. The military attitude was to get the job done, and this meant, in its view, reliance upon big business. In the words of the chief of Army Service Forces and Commanding General of the Services of Supply, Brehon Somervell, "all the small plants of the country could not turn out one day's requirements of ammunition."[33]

The truth or falsity of the statement has never been adequately examined, but the attitude contained in it no doubt undermined the small business procurement effort.

One way of appraising those results is to look at the official procurement record. That record shows: of $175 billion of prime contracts awarded between June 1940 and September 1944, over one-half went to the top 33 corporations (with size measured by value of prime contracts received). The smallest 94 percent of prime supply contract corporations (contracts of $9 million or less) got 10 percent of the value of all prime contracts in that period.[34] With regard to subcontracts, a 1943 survey by the SWPC found that a group of 252 of the largest contracting corporations subcontracted about a third of the value of their prime contracts, but three-fourths of that went to other large (over 500 employees) concerns.[35] The third Annual Report of the Senate Special Committee to Investigate the National Defense Program (the Truman Committee) stated that "the 100 corporations having the largest contracts for war materials held approximately 70 percent of the total amount of prime war-supply contracts reported in the period June 1940–September 1943. This should be contrasted with the 30 percent of civilian business which such corporations held before the war."[36] The following tabulation of the number and dollar value of contracts later awarded by government procurement agencies provides a partial overall view of the smaller firms' share for the peak years of the war production effort:[37]

	1943	1944
total contracts, number	241,531	163,114
total value, $ billions	35.3	24.8
under 100 wage earners		
percent of number	35.7	29.2
percent of value	3.5	5.5
under 500 earners:		
percent of number	62.8	59.6
percent of value	12.6	20.6

It can be calculated, for example, that the smallest group of firms (or establishments) was awarded about 86,000 contracts in the peak year 1943. Clearly, some progress was made in terms of numbers under the small business program. The share by value, of course, was extremely small.

The historical estimates of the number of manufacturing firms in operation, the overwhelming bulk of which are always small, show 221,000 in 1939 and 246,000 in 1944.[38] This 11 percent increase may be compared with the SWPC estimates of 204,000 firms in July–September 1939 and 218,000 in October–December 1944,[39] a 7 percent rise. Neither of these percentages are large for a period in which manufacturing production expanded over 100 percent. Small manufacturing firms with less than 100 employees accounted for about 26 percent of total manufacturing employment in December 1939, but this share had declined to only 19 percent five years later.[40] This reduction occurred in the context of a 55 percent jump in total manufacturing employment over the same period. It was the biggest firms that gained, and the gain was tremendous: those with 10,000 employees or more employed 13 percent of all manufacturing workers in December 1939, but they employed over 30 percent in December 1944'[41] World War II apparently weakened the market position of the small firm segment of the manufacturing sector.[42]

Small Manufacturing and Reconversion

As the pace of military procurement reached a plateau in 1944 and slowly wound down from the manufacturing employment peak of November 1943, the competition got under way to reconvert after further expected military contract terminations,[43] and to be among the first to grab postwar civilian markets. Again, the champions of the small manufacturing firm (defined as one with fewer than 500 employees) in the Congress and the wartime executive agencies, with varying degrees of vigor, came to the fore with demands for fair small business market shares on grounds of both equity and protection of the "free enterprise" system against the likely encroachments of the oligopolies.

Throughout 1944, until the temporary German breakthrough of Allied lines (Battle of the Bulge) on December 16, the controversy over help for small business raged between the mild reconversionists led by Donald Nelson and his group on WPB, the Senate and House Small Business Committees, the Truman Committee, and Maury Maverick of SWPC on the one side, and on the opposition side the Joint Chiefs of Staff, the Services of Supply, certain high-ups such as Charles Edward Wilson of General Electric on WPB, the War Manpower Commission under Paul V. McNutt, and Director James F. Byrnes of the plenary Office of War Mobilization.

As early as February 22, 1944, Byrnes had publicly announced that 3,769 army prime contract terminations were already creating reconversion problems.[44] Nelson's most controversial response to the anticipation of further cutbacks was the issuance of the modest WPB Priorities Regulation 25 that permitted regional Offices of the board to authorize, after consultation with the WMC, production of certain items where plants were fulfilling their military contracts and/or experienced cutbacks, provided war production in the particular labor market area did not require the idle workers. This moderate reconversion order, "PR 25," was issued in June 1944, the month of the Allied invasion of Western Europe. It became the focal point of the Armed Services' attack on reconversion for the next year. While the services had no legal grounds for interfering with PR 25, it must be remembered that wartime Washington, and Byrnes's agency in particular, never resolved the incredible administrative clash between a WPB responsible for total production and an armed forces' establishment endowed with, and acutely jealous of,[45] its authority over military procurement.

The latter authority, abetted by a malicious propaganda war, was decisive in a bitter conflict that raged from June 1944 until after V-E Day. The defeat of Nelson and his allies by the developing big business—military coalition, despite the steady rise in War Department contract terminations both in numbers and in value of commitments throughout 1944 and continuing into 1945,[46] may be encapsulated by the Brewster Aeronautical Corporation story. Termination of the corporation's contract for navy fighter planes on May 22, 1944, with only one day's notification to the WPB, three days to the Brewster officials, and less to the 9,000 surprised workers, led to a vain "stay-in strike," denial of the firm's request for materials authorizations for civilian appliance production, closure of its Long Island City plant, and the auction sale of all its tools, equipment, and parts.[47]

A national policy of deliberately creating general unemployment became familiar in the anti-inflation crusade of the 1970s. In 1944, however, the "tradeoff" that was presumed to justify local pools of human unemployment was weakened "civilian morale," unwanted and premature optimism," aggravation of an alleged ordnance "shortage," and the danger of an increased stimulation of labor turnover and absenteeism. But in neither situation was there widespread public discussion of any obligation to the human victims of such government policies. In 1944 and early 1945 it was simplistically assumed by the Armed Services not only that there were serious "shortage" areas but that humans, like materials, could or would move from surplus to alleged shortage areas with inconsequential "frictions."

This view was sometimes presented in extreme and even dishonest forms. For example, Henry J. Kaiser, one of the entrepreneurial heroes of the war, announced in November 1944 that the war effort was being imperiled by workers quitting vital jobs and that his West Coast shipyards were "losing men so fast that it is becoming very critical; in the Richmond yard alone, we lost about 26,000 workers."[48] The report was widely circulated as part of the propaganda war of the army and the WMC; but a check on the alleged 26,000 lost employees revealed that those workers had been laid off because of reduced production schedules![49]

In the midst of this feud Senator Truman publicly charged that reconversion was being delayed by "some selfish business groups that want to see their competition kept idle . . . [and] by Army and Navy representatives who want to create a surplus of manpower . . . "[50] Senator James M. Mead told the Senate as late as December 16, 1944, the day the Battle of the Bulge opened, that

There has been a misconception of the problem. Insufficient production in the United States has not up to this time been the cause of the shortage of weapons and ammunition at the front . . . Unfortunately certain news stories concerning actual shortages of ammunition in the hands of our fighting men have carried the implication that the lack of cartridges and ammunition at the front was due to some failure of production at home. These implications, we are assured, were not intended, and they are not well-founded.[51]

Mead's reference to assurances was solidly based in part upon statements of General Brehon B. Somervell himself, who nonetheless a short time previously had publicly sounded an alarm regarding alleged production lags. [52]

The results of the reconversion controversy, as illustrated by the subsequent severe curtailment of PR 25's spot authorization program, [53] were to provide (much like conversion) only a few crumbs for small business. There followed a similarly heated conflict during 1945–46 over the questions of a fair share for small manufacturing with respect to the disposition of government-owned surplus products and war plants, and, after V-J Day, WPB decontrol of supplies of scarce raw materials and industrial components.

Given prevailing attitudes strongly partial to private possession and operation of industry, together with a significant anti–New Deal reassertion of the traditional abhorrence of government intervention in economic affairs, transfer to private business of between $15 and $17 billion of government-owned plant and equipment was inevitable. The publicly owned plant, sited in such industries as aircraft, chemicals, steel, aluminum, copper, and shipbuilding, was estimated to be about 15 percent of the total postwar plant capacity. [54] In addition, it was believed that the amount of "surplus" property amounted to between $50 and $70 billion. [55]

What was significant for small business with respect to the publicly owned plants was the fact that the financing conditions under which the plants had been constructed included the promise that the private firms operating them would be given the opportunity to purchase them at war's end should they choose to do so. This proviso contributed to forestalling acquisition by competitors, large and small. Hence the distribution of wartime operating controls over the $11.6 billion of industrial facilities operated by private concerns decisively shaped the immediate postwar small enterprise acquisition opportunities. That distributive pattern, of course, was shaped in large part initially by the financing decisions of the Defense Plant Corporation, a subsidiary of the Reconstruction Finance Corporation; the War and Navy departments; and the Maritime Commission—none of which had shown great interest in the effects on postwar market structure of those decisions. War plant financing pretty much followed the concentrated pattern of prime military contract distribution; indeed, concentration with respect to the former exceeded the highly concentrated prime contract awards.[56] About 83 percent of the value of the privately operated, publicly financed industrial facilities (excluding management-fee extensions of the government's arsenal system and directly government operated facilities) were operated by only 168 corporations; and the hundred largest corporations operated three-fourths of the value of government-owned facilities.[57] Of course, the few industries most heavily involved were typically oligopolistic, and opportunities for "small enterprise" entry were never bright. Also, at least 70 percent by value of the government plants had cost more than $10 million each.[58] Hence there was a sharp inconsistency between the professed public purpose of affording small firms an opportunity to acquire war plants (and surplus property) on equal terms with larger competitors on the one hand, and the equally avowed aim of refraining from unduly disturbing established market positions on the other. In the prominent case of aluminum,[59] the prewar monopoly of aluminum ingot production by the Aluminum Company of America was broken in January 1946, but the government's disposal of its owned or financed aluminum facilities under the October 1944 Surplus Property Act to Reynolds Metals and Kaiser Aluminum created a dominant-firm oligopoly in ingot production. The oligopolistic outcome of the Surplus Property Board's plant disposal program of selling at the highest distress prices possible has been termed a "debacle" for small enterprise by one industrial organization specialist. He noted that about two-thirds (by "value") of the $17 billion of government plant and equipment at war's end was sold to 87 large firms, that "the bulk of copolymer synthetic rubber plants went to the Big Four in rubber; large chemical plants were sold to the leading oil companies; and U.S. Steel received 71 per cent of government-built integrated steel plants."[60]

In the case of raw and semifinished materials, the war's end brought a quick upsurge in civilian demand for consumption commodities and fixed capital goods, and a consequent scramble by all business for raw-stuffs in general and usable government surplus property in particular. In the context of the resultant shortages, a policy of hasty decontrol created grave concern on the part of Economic Stabilization Director Chester Bowles, Maury Maverick of the SWPC, and the Office of

Price Administration, that prices would skyrocket and small businesses would experience severe deprivation of supplies as big firms grabbed most of what was available.[61] However, under the impulsive leadership of WPB chairman Julius Krug, a policy of rapid decontrol was pursued after V-E Day, and by November 3, 1945, only 50 some control orders remained of the wartime peak of 650.[62] It is noteworthy, as pointed out by Barton Bernstein, that even liberals supported decontrol and release of surplus construction materials because they feared a postwar slump and therefore desired a quick expansion of housing construction materials to provide an offsetting stimulus.[63] It is also noteworthy that, whereas small business consequently got no help from retention of WPB controls over materials and little help in the disposition of surplus property, it generally did not make its voice heard in support of Bowles and Maverick.[64]

Thus ended the saga of war period planning efforts to defend the market position of small manufacturing enterprise. It has already been noted that it fared none too well in the war years 1941–45. Its growth was inhibited. It would appear, however, that some of the fear for the fate of the small manufacturer during reconversion was exaggerated. The return to peace meant a great drop in manufacturing production; and the bottom was reached in 1946, when the output index had returned to approximately the level of 1941. The subsequent production rise to the cyclical peak of 1953 was in excess of 50 percent, a condition ordinarily favorable for new entry and the proliferation of smaller concerns over an intermediate time period. Indeed, this is what happened. The total number of firms in manufacturing rose from 264,000 to 331,000, or one-fourth, between 1946 and 1953, a substantial increase. The bulk of these were undoubtedly small, for between 1947 and 1954 both establishments with less than 20 employees and establishments in single-plant firms also increased about one-fourth.[65] This peacetime intermediate-period recovery was of course running parallel with the long-run contraction of the small manufacturer's market space: the share of total manufacturing real value added accounted for by the single-plant firms declined from 41 to 32 percent between 1947 and 1954, and had dropped to 17 percent by the late seventies (1977). Alternatively put, 255,000 single-plant firms were sharing the small real total of value added in 1954 that 206,000 had shared seven years earlier.[66]

Chapter Four

Wartime Administration

GOVERNMENT GUIDANCE at the start of the war was greatly facilitated by the huge preparedness apparatus that had already been initiated. Although the new wartime administrative organism suffered the usual growing pains—the staff of the WPB grew from the 6,600 it inherited in January 1942 to 18,000 on the following July 1—it enjoyed a momentum of inestimable value for the enormous and heartrending tasks that lay ahead. The mobilization bureaucracy had been a useful preparatory school for dealing with many essentially similar problems that abided throughout the war years.

To be sure, that bureaucracy had learned less than it might about a government-directed economy of vested interest groups. It could have learned much more about how to organize its own household. Also, administrators always had to wrestle with the conflict within themselves between the public interest (when known) and the interest of the particular group, sector, or industry for which they were responsible. Furthermore, the preparedness bureaucracy had the difficult task of transmitting the knowledge it had acquired to a much larger, sprawling, heterogeneous army of neophyte controllers.

While participation in the war came by no means as a complete surprise to the mobilizers in Washington, and while they but dimly comprehended the magnitude of the upcoming administrative job, they eventually fashioned a functioning organization that helped guide the way to victory. Neither the private market alone, nor the private market in collaboration with the War and Navy departments, could possibly have produced the spectacular American economic contribution to Axis defeat.

There was no great operational war agency dealing with the economy that lacked a pre–Pearl Harbor predecessor of some kind. There were name changes, reorganizations, and much jurisdictional jockeying, but continuity was a distinctive feature of the main parts of the apparatus. Within that framework, the war years continued to bring forth new administrative bodies to try to coordinate the parts of the machine. It was the same as it had been under preparedness: the constituent, administratively separated agencies were struggling segmentally to give or hinder direction toward an interconnected system. As War Production Board Chairman Donald Nelson surprisingly insisted once in the heat of an administrative conflict, no workable means had yet been developed for making a boundary between the military and the civilian sectors of an indivisible national economy: "this civilian economy is not a portion or segment, of the total economy—but it is the entire economy."[1] Of course, the denial of the existence of economic sectors is as pointless as failure to acknowledge their interdependence.

The new controlling apparatus endeavored to represent, through a mixture of departmentalization and coordination, this functional interconnectedness of the economy in the face of nonrecognition, ignorance, inexperience, misunderstanding, poor communication, personal rivalries, and departmental self-aggrandizement. But now the struggle for administrative efficiency was blessed with a foreboding sense of national unity for very survival. Administrators could henceforth count on the full support of the public—within the constraint of widespread customary preference for minimal interference with the private market.

Until May 1943 the super civilian surveillance agency remained exclusively the Office for Emergency Management. While OEM continued to live through the war, the establishment of the paramount civilian war agency, the War Production Board, in the month after Pearl Harbor began to relegate the OEM to the more remote role of "a sort of super administrative services division" for the other war-directing organizations.[2] The OEM never evolved into a central co-ordinating body for actual operations.[3]

The economics of the war at home entailed the battle of production, distribution, pricing, and fiscal policy. The control agencies were constructed around the first three of these, and they were the ones dismantled at war's end. The essentials of the wartime fiscal program were not dismantled because they were an intrinsic component of the fiscal revolution at the heart of the future mixed economy.

The important departments of the economy constituting the production of goods and services, and facilities devoted to them, were addressed by the administrative giant, the WPB, which replaced the OPM and the SPAB. The jurisdictional design for the board encompassed the production of all finished capital goods and materials, military goods, and consumer products, with the notable exclusions of food, housing, and transportation.

By designating Donald M. Nelson of Sears, Roebuck sole chairman of the WPB, the President relinquished his reluctance to delegate power to a single head; and at the same time he demoted Sidney Hillman from his position as coordinate chief of the mobilization program. Nelson appointed Hillman as director of the board's Labor Division on January 26, 1942, but even in this second-tier prestige position Hillman was to have a comparatively short ride.[4]

Labor was as essential as plant and matériel for production, and indeed as the numbers in uniform mounted, the labor shortage, not severe in 1942, became an ever more pressing problem long after the provision of facilities was largely solved. Labor supply, viewed as a department of the economy, was assigned to the independent War Manpower Commission, which in April 1942 took over the regulatory responsibilities formerly assumed by the Labor Division of the OPM. Significantly, the WMC was headed by Paul V. McNutt of the Federal Security Agency, not by Sidney Hillman. The new commission was instructed to coordinate with the WPB's Labor Requirements Committee—a perfectly reasonable, necessary liaison arrangement; but a zone of jurisdictional differences was thereby created.

The civilian-military tug-of-war also typified the WMC's coordinative and operational functioning. Between the time of its establishment within the OEM and the end of 1942 the commission was quite ineffective and without its own field organization. Central to its infirmity as an operating agency were two obstructive influences: the first was the fact that both business and labor believed, with considerable justification at the moment, that the large available labor pool and the market mechanism could manage that year's bottleneck problems; the second was the established labor placement capability of the U.S. Employment Service. Both the Employment Service, nominally under WMC control by executive order, and the Selective Service,[5] each in their separate ways, had been busy drafting, deferring, and processing and placing workers. Neither saw any reason for relinquishing their activities to a mere coordinating body. The Employment Service acted as WMC's major operating arm throughout the war, an arrangement that overcame to a great extent the debilitating effect of the fact that the commission's directives lacked the force of law—it had to depend upon persuasion backed up by the image of authority and the patriotism of workers.

From 1943 on the chief administrative deficiency in the national labor program was the separation of, and conflicts over, the tasks of recruitment and deferment for the armed forces (Selective Service), versus recruitment and occupational deferment for the production process. The resultant jurisdictional problems were further cluttered up administratively by the intervention of the succession of labor divisions (under various names) within the WPB. The President's Executive Order of December 5, 1942, designed to convert WMC into an operating agency with a formal mandate to control both civilian and military recruitment, made it possible in 1943 for the commission to develop a field organization. From then on until the agency's termination in September 1945 there had to be, and there was, much more cooperation between the different labor administrations. That cooperation helped forestall the adoption of a national service law (compulsory labor conscription), for which there had been considerable agitation.

The obstructions to interagency coordination throughout the control network were compounded by the proliferation of independent control organizations. A case in point was the activities of the Petroleum Administration for War (established December 1942), which in 1943 was prohibiting the movement of gasoline by tank cars to the East

Coast at the very time the OPA planned to remove its current ban on personal automobile use.[6] Again, in June 1943 there was a tussle between the Office of Defense Transportation (established December 18, 1941) and the Petroleum Administration, when the "Czar" heading the former agency insisted that the responsibility for determination of petroleum requirements for all transportation services lay clearly in his office.[7] In mid-1943, a conflict arose over coal rationing methods between OPA and a "commodity czar" agency, the Solid Fuels Administration, the OPA, and the Office of Defense Transportation.[8]

The czar agencies were "final demanders" among about thirteen "claimant agencies," so named because they had top-ranking (and of course often competing) claims on finished output, materials, and facilities required for their respective economic sectors. The National Housing Agency (established February 1942) was a critical claimant, as was the Maritime Commission, which was responsible for ship-building. Ocean shipping was administered by a czar heading the War Shipping Administration. So also was the Foreign Economic Administration, established in September 1943 as a consolidation of all former agencies, such as the Lend-Lease Administration and the Board of Economic Warfare, operating in the foreign field. Of course, the dominant claimant agencies were the army and navy, jointly represented by the Army-Navy Munitions Board (ANMB).

Administrative Coordination Problems

The organizations so far discussed, designed to deal with the allocation of scarce/strategic/critical labor and products, constituted the core of the wartime administrative apparatus for production. A central problem of control resided in separated and overlapping functions inherent in the structure of that apparatus. This hindered the coordination of defense programming under the OPM. The same disjointedness obtained in wartime with the WPB, which was in its conception designed to be the nerve center of war production controls.

Yet WPB's powers were curtailed at its inception, in part by the concurrent existence or the fresh creation of other ostensibly authoritative agencies, such as the czar agencies, outside its purview. This state of affairs obtained preeminently, of course, with respect to the dominant claimant agencies, army, navy, Maritime Commission, the air forces, and the Foreign Economic Administration. As another example, labor power allocation, without which no production could occur, was under the aegis of the WMC. Furthermore, at the outset of its career the WPB voluntarily yielded up to the Armed Services both priorities power and the right to clear military contracts *before* the contracts were let to suppliers. Such abdication of power by the WPB (in its General Administrative Orders nos. 2-23 and 2-33 in March and April 1942) surrendered direct decision-making authority over the great bulk of the finished output needed for war.

This renouncement by WPB Chairman Donald Nelson was, of course, just what the services wanted—to direct production themselves. The board's administrative order in March stipulated that the War Department, through the Services of Supply and the Army Air Forces, was to carry on "its supply functions of research, design, development, programming, purchase, production, storage, distribution, issue, maintenance, and salvage."[9] A similar agreement with the Navy Department was added in the April order.

Armed with such a hunting license, the services proceeded to freely trespass upon the territory the President had assigned to the WPB. The war history of the Bureau of the Budget described the ensuing production control relationship as "a running fight between the War Department and the War Production Board which was to continue for several years."[10] A rough division of labor did eventuate. The Services of Supply assumed the ultimate decision-making power over all finished goods, leaving more or less to the WPB the domain of vital raw materials and semifinished products.[11]

One immediate result was an enormous inflation in contracts, and even in matériel and plant construction, in 1942—an unplanned mixture leaving a residue of surpluses and shortages in particular lines, and putting some sectors of the civilian economy in jeopardy toward years' end:

Locomotive plants went into tank production when locomotives were more necessary than tanks . . . Truck plants began to produce airplanes, a change that caused shortages of trucks later on . . . Merchant ships took steel from the Navy, and the landing craft cut into both. The Navy took aluminum from aircraft. Rubber took valves from escort vessels, from petroleum, from the Navy. The pipe-lines took steel from ships, new tools, and the railroads. And at every turn there were foreign demands to be met as well as requirements for new plants . . .

We built many new factories, and expanded many others [continues this official defense of Nelson's regime which documents his downfall as few exposés could], which we could not use and did not need. Many of these new factories we could not supply with labor or with raw materials, or if we had, we would not have been able to fly the planes or shoot the ammunition that would come out of them. But in the process we used up critical material which might better have gone into something else . . . The Services were equipped with high priorities, which gave the contractors confidence that they would be able to get the materials and components they required, price arrangements were generous and elastic, and the manufacturers were not unwilling, under pressure, to sign additional contracts even when their plants were already full, hoping to expand, or to find some other method of discharging their inflated obligations. With this combination of circumstances, over $100 billion of contracts were placed in the first six months of 1942. In other words, industry signed up to deliver for war more than the total production of the American economy in the Nation's most prosperous and productive prior year. At the time, there were also some $20 billions of orders outstanding, mostly for munitions, $12.6 billions for industrial expansion, and $6.9 billions for military construction.[12]

This passage from the Budget Bureau history is quoted at some length because it reveals not merely some of the unfortunate effects of the WPB's precipitate and ill-considered transfer of authority, but also and mainly because it depicts the anarchic pattern of behavior that was likely to be associated with the unfettered exercise of bountiful buying power by the Armed Services. It was fortunate that the tremendous capabilities of the U.S. economy made possible the provision of minimal military needs in numerous items.

As was also characteristic of the services, their contract allocations concentrated both the procurement orders and discretion over their execution in the hands of the largest private corporations, leaving the WPB's Smaller War Plants Division and Congress' small business subcontracting program to fight a rear-guard action.

In almost every case the WPB—in addition to its operationally powerful commodity and industry divisions, which actually handled most of the board's workload of programming and supervising the production of basic metals and other materials—created divisions paralleling the responsibilities assigned to the czar agencies. Cases in point were the WPB's Controller of Shipbuilding and Shipbuilding Division, Labor Production Division, Manpower Requirements Division, and the Division of International Supply. While it was true that the board needed to be involved in these matters, the powerful divisions became a part of a whole nexus of counterpart jurisdictions afflicted with continued confusion and widespread legitimate doubts about who had what authority.

The Civilian Supply Sector

The wartime supervision over civilian supply was a perpetual orphan in the administrative population, and the provision of civilian goods was treated as a poor relation. It was fortunate that in the crucial year 1942 the military, in spite of the flood of contracts, left the civilian economy initially in a situation of adequate residual supply. The Armed Services followed a policy of scrambling for their requirements essentially without clearing with the WPB and without much regard for the impact on the civilian economy.

In addition to attitudinal blockages against the civilian sector, the administrative hierarchy was a fragmented labyrinth. The WPB had its Civilian Supply Division, then its Office of Civilian Supply (OCS); and later, as of May 1943 a claimant called Office of Civilian Requirements, under OPA chief Leon Henderson, assisted by the able Joseph L. Weiner, which was responsible for "programming" non-military production. It had a unit designed to help provide housing for war workers by assuring priorities assistance and materials allocation to the National Housing Agency, and it had Industry Divisions presumed to facilitate appropriately the flow of consumer products. The OPA was also concerned with the civilian supplies by virtue of its rationing duties. The Office of Civilian Supply of the WPB voiced a lament at the board's meeting in January 1943 that sounded strikingly similar to that of Leon Henderson regarding OPA and the czar organizations, mentioned above. Its director complained that

The establishment of uncoordinated "czars" in the various commodities emphasizes the need for a strong coordinating agency to represent civilian interests. He stated that the Office of Civilian Supply has had no representation in the field of food . . . In the field of fuel, the Office of Civilian Supply is not representing civilian interests. The Rubber Director has taken the position that he, and not the Office of Civilian Supply, shall represent civilian interests in the allocation of rubber . . . unless an over-all representative capacity is assigned to civilian supply there can be no integrated programming for the civilian economy.[13]

WPB Chairman Donald Nelson added that the OCS did not have adequate representation in the field of manpower, either. There were also coordination problems between the board's Office of Civilian Requirements and its own Industry Divisions.

The board's civilian supply unit suffered a demotion as compared with the OPM-SPAB period because it was now merely a staff planning and programming body, not an operating agency.[14] Its duties were to plan, collect data, inform, and advise other WPB divisions and outside agencies in pursuance of its two-pronged objective, the curtailment of nonessentials and the furtherance of the production interests of the civilian population.

In the early months of its existence the Division of Civilian Supply was legitimately much concerned with the definition of its duties and with the already time-worn issue, what did civilian requirements mean? Not much clarity was added to the answer by midyear, when the staff decided its scope encompassed "indirect military" as well as minimum civilian requirements.[15] Unfortunately, the unit's responsibility regarding rationing of civilian goods was unclear and never formally stated.[16] There was in fact no comprehensive central planning or administration for the civilian sector in 1943 and even by 1944–45, although, over the continued fierce objections of the Armed Services, that sector was gradually given more attention by both the Congress and the various control bodies. Scrutiny and revision of WMC's essential activities list was elicited. Attention also had to be paid to those subsectors in which there were severe shortages, such as durables, fuels, housing, and the chronic tire shortage which was critical enough to require the introduction of the seven-day work week as late as March 1945. Food and farm supplies were of course a special case because the vociferous pressure of Agriculture's War Food Administration wrung concessions again and again, even from some of the military claimants at times.

As time passed and the squeeze on the civilian sector intensified, the Civilian Requirements unit pressed ever more vigorously for protection of the civilian sector. Its emphasis shifted from needed sacrifices by civilians to the fulfillment of their essential needs.[17] In 1944 the Office of Civilian Requirements busied itself with consumer surveys and with setting up essentiality lists and levels of requirements for the civilian sector. Indeed, the office ultimately elevated itself into the position of consumer advocate, a much needed role in view of the usual presumptuousness attributed to any civilian claimant that challenged the Armed Services' assertions of military necessity. Of course, there was always the background factor with which Civilian Requirements had to cope: everyone knew that the American consumer was in general not suffering great material hardship at any time during the war.

Drummond Jones has ably summarized the major administrative problems with which the civilian supply agencies had to deal throughout the defense and war period:

The early tendency of the civilian supply organization to neglect its real role, becoming in its insistence on industrial conversion for war as much a military needs group as the Services themselves; the eventual recognition that civilians could yield no more of their resources on a wholesale basis, and the ensuing measuring of the relative strengths of advocates of military and civilian needs; the inability of the production agency to prevent incursions by the Armed Services on civilian needs when that would have meant exercise of judgment on strategic matters; the difficulty in distinguishing true strategic needs of the Services from less urgent stated requirements of the Services; the difficulty of persuading the Services that munitions production depended upon a genuinely healthy economy during a long war effort; the difficulties encountered in attempts to calculate civilian needs statistically; the danger that goods produced for civilian use under approved programs might actually be acquired by Service procurement officers; the question of effectiveness of the Office of Civilian Requirements in integrating its activities and programs with WPB's operations in industry; the uncertainties as to the readiness of WPB's industry divisions to execute approved civilian programs; the position of the Office of Civilian Requirements with respect to the removal of industrial controls at war's end; and the sharp clash of personalities concerned with the solution of these and other problems.[18]

It will be noticed that a number of Jones' points have relevance for interagency relationships that go beyond the civilian requirements field to the general case of coordination problems throughout the control bureaucracy.

Activities of the War Production Board

It was noted above that the work of the WPB in the raw and sem-ifinished materials field was its major concentration and also probably represented its chief contribution to the war production effort. In mid-1942 the board concluded that conversion had been substantially completed and that a new emphasis upon assuring the production and distribution of the already very short supply of rawstuffs was in order.[19] Under the consequent "July realignment" of the board, the industry branches were directed to become the "primary contact of the WPB with industry and the common meeting ground of business, government and labor [sic] through which American production will be geared to war."[20]

The result of this realignment was not only the elevation of industry divisions to the driver's seat in the WPB, but also the reactivation of the "production requirements plan" (PRP) for an integrated materials distribution control system that had been inaugurated in a loose form and on a voluntary basis as early as December 1941. Already in May 1942 the board had made PRP a mandatory program in place of its previous blanket priority rating orders. Up to the time when the board issued its June 10th Regulation no. 11 requiring any firm using more than $5,000 of critical metals to get PRP clearance if it wanted materials, "war material was being produced, but war production was not being administered."[21] PRP was a great step toward rational, centralized organization, prompted by the growing crisis in raw materials. The need for synthetic rubber was a case in point.

But by late November of the same year a more intensive system of materials controls seemed to be required, and in consequence Chairman Nelson announced inauguration of the Controlled Materials Plan (CMP), with particular but not exclusive reference to the initial metals. Materials would henceforth be allotted "vertically," replacing PRP's horizontal allocations by product classification. WPB was itself reorganized to conform with the well-planned CMP.[22] There followed a transition period, and CMP as an elaborate mandatory reporting system and programming technique did not go into effect until the third quarter of 1943. Under CMP the claimant agencies allotted materials to prime contractors, with WPB approval, who then suballotted to their suppliers.[23] CMP became the backbone of production readjustments in military procurement and in the modest amount of civilian production programming undertaken by the WPB. The CMP thus became "the central instrument for adjustment of production programs in accordance with strategic requirements and the prospective supply of critical resources."[24] The focal role assumed by WPB's industry divisions and the newly created Controlled Materials Plan Division will be apparent.

Labor-Management Controls

The National War Labor Board (WLB), created in January 1942, assumed full wartime responsibility for wage stabilization and for the labor-management relations work formerly conducted by the National Defense Mediation Board. The WLB began its work under the favorable circumstance of the no-strike, no-lookout pledge made by labor and business at a conference called by the President in mid-December of 1941. Its major function in the industrial relations field was to prevent disputes referred to it by the Secretary of Labor from obstructing essential war production. Labor, management, and the perennial "public" were represented equally on the board. It was given explicit authority to require arbitration of a dispute if deemed necessary, but if a dispute did not interfere with war production it was allowed to stay in mediation. In making its decision the board was required to conform to the provisions of the Fair Labor Standards Act of 1938 and the National Labor Relations Act.

Throughout the war the board was able to draw upon the expertise and general services of the National Labor Relations Board, with whom it maintained basically harmonious relationships.[25] Its enforcement powers were great: in addition to the ultimate threat of government seizure and operation via referral to the President it could request the War Department to cancel contracts or blacklist, request WPB to deny priority, or refer a case to the Bureau of Internal Revenue for disallowance of tax deductions for wages paid in violation of its orders.[26]

While some other agencies infringed upon its activities at times, the WLB's career was stormy because of rising industrial unrest, not because of interagency conflicts. The board risked and received over time the hostility of labor because it administered compliance with wage stabilization goals in the face of rising prices and carried out the provisions of the hated Smith-Connally Antistrike Act of June 1943. It incurred the hostility of business because it circumvented the money-wage restrictions of the Little Steel Formula (see chapter 5) by opening the fringe-benefit floodgates; upheld equal wages for women for comparable work; removed intraplant wage inequities; and favored uniform wage rate structures, union maintenance of membership agreements, and settlements protecting the closed or union shop.

The board's life became ever more harassed as its fringe benefit concessions lagged behind the moderate price creep in 1943 and 1944, and its mounting caseload brought delays in the consideration of disputes. The CIO coal miners' strikes in the summer of 1943 under John L. Lewis created a crisis for the board, when Lewis refused to acknowledge what he considered its biased authority. When a final settlement was reluctantly approved by the board (while the mines were still in government possession), the miners had won their portal-to-portal pay demand. Meanwhile, the number of work stoppages mounted steadily, but few would attribute that trend to the bias or incompetency of a Labor Board that had executed a generally very successful experiment in tripartite labor-management relations under most trying conditions. The *Termination Report* of the board pointed out that in over 95 percent of the 17,650 dispute cases it closed, the decision resolved the dispute without further threat to production.[27]

Throughout the years of preparation and wartime involvement, attempts were made, largely at organized labor's behest, to institutionalize joint labor-management direction of the defense/war effort. Organized labor wanted wartime representation and participation in production decision-making at all levels, not merely the meaningless advisory role allotted to it during the preparedness period. But from the outset, management maintained a chronic hostile stance on the ground that management-labor industry councils such as proposed by Walter Reuther and CIO President Philip Murray in 1940 would, under cover of patriotism, undermine management's prerogatives and inaugurate a postwar "sovietization" of American industry.

The pressure from labor succeeded in inducing Donald Nelson to set up in March 1942 a special War Production Drive Division in WPB to encourage the voluntary establishment across the country of joint labor-management plant committees to raise production and efficiency.[28] Murray promptly elicited employer and WPB paranoia about the drive by announcing that it was "directly in line with the CIO's Industry Council proposals."[29] Employer fears were allayed by WPB action, however, separating the Drive Division from the WPB Labor Division, instructing the plant committees to confine themselves to "physical production problems," and forbidding them to deal with standard collective bargaining issues.[30] The several thousand resultant plant committees helped to forestall labor participation in production planning at levels higher than the plant, to restrict the joint activities to minor employee problems of aid to employers, to stimulate greater worker effort on the job, and to further patriotic drives and campaigns. The largest firms in several basic industries even refused to allow the committees in their plants. Few committees survived the war.

Fresh Efforts at Coordination: The Office of War Mobilization

In taking stock of the whole wartime administrative structure in midstream 1943, it became ever more apparent to both Congress and the war administration that much tighter overall governmental coordination of production was by far the most pressing operational need. To be sure, considerable advances in this respect had been achieved.

The exceptionally comprehensive CMP was an example, but that was integrated planning in only one particular sphere, just as the Office of Economic Stabilization (OES), established October 3, 1942, had done successful coordinating work, but in a vague sphere nominally confined to controls over the cost of living, civilian purchasing power, and "unnecessary migration" of labor. As for the WPB, while it had been partially successful as an integrative agency in its own sphere, it certainly fell short of being a central directing organization for the whole war production effort, a shortfall for which it was by no means wholly responsible.

The Subcommittee on War Mobilization of the Senate Committee on Military Affairs declared in mid-May 1943 that war mobilization was in a state of crisis, and urged immediate administrative action to cope with the problems.[31] The Truman Investigation Committee had for some time been pressing for the creation of a new top-level agency with centralized authority.[32] These were the actions of a restive Congress that was concerned also about the concentration of wartime administrative power in the hands of the executive. However, the latter again took the initiative, and by Executive Order established on May 27, 1943, the Office of War Mobilization (OWM), of which James F. Byrnes, whom Eliot Janeway has characterized as Assistant President in charge of not rocking the boat, was made director.[33] Byrnes immediately followed custom by appointing an Advisory Board.

The new nonoperating superagency for policy, added as it was to the top of the existing administrative apparatus proceeded to begin a considerable reduction in the status of the WPB, except for WPB's sacrosanct Industry Divisions. In the administrative hierarchy the OWM was placed at the same level as the Office for Emergency Management, and over the WPB. OWM's sweeping directive was to

develop unified programs and to establish policies for the maximum use of the nation's natural and industrial resources for military and civilian needs, for the effective use of the national manpower not in the Armed Forces, for the maintenance and stabilization of the civilian economy, and for the adjustment of such economy to war needs and conditions.[34]

It will be observed at once that in the policy statement total production, civilian labor power, and the civilian economy were all properly linked together conceptually. Furthermore, there was explicit reference in the Executive Order to the unification of the activities and reduction of the controversies between the various federal war agencies concerned with production, procurement, and the distribution and transport of military and civilian supplies, materials, and products. Two months after the OWM was created its jurisdiction was extended to the international economic field.[35]

Despite its tiny staff, OWM was destined to be a great leap forward in wartime policy planning for production. For one thing, the dynamic Byrnes was given a great deal of power, with an office in the White House. He was both a disciple of the President and an experienced strategist. Among other appropriate moves, he coopted Bernard Baruch to act as a consultant to OWM, during which tenure Baruch and his assistant John Hancock prepared their famous report on *War and Post-War Adjustment Policies.* Byrnes's office perspicaciously conducted planning at the agency level, using the agency staffs themselves to coordinate and execute programs, rather than building up a huge organization of its own. Its success in so proceeding was underpinned by OWM's insistence upon safeguarding the autonomy of the particular operating agency.

As Byrnes's leadership role evolved, his office made substantial contributions to integrating the work of the WPB and the WMC in spite of a good deal of resistance from Donald Nelson, who frequently viewed such coordination as a threat to the presumed hegemony of his jurisdiction—as indeed it had to be. "The status of the War Production Board tended to deteriorate in 1944 as the actual center of power shifted" to the WMC, the agency responsible at that juncture in the war for the most critical production resource—labor power.[36] Through much of 1944

WPB found itself an equal, rather than a superior, of the agencies represented around its own council tables. WPB could not act contrary to the firm views of such agencies as the Armed Services and the War Manpower Commission without inviting an appeal to higher authority. And that higher authority was often the Director of War Mobilization rather than the President.[37]

Byrnes's office also initiated a strategy entailing continuous review and coordination of the several procurement programs of the War and Navy Departments.

The OWM was quite generally successful in making itself the locus of decisions where interagency conflicts needed to be resolved.[38] The War Department tended to accept OWM as final arbiter in its own differences with other agencies.[39] Byrnes put a stop to the military agencies' practice of looking only to the Joint Chiefs of Staff for ultimate procurement decisions.[40]

The Office of Economic Stabilization continued its work as an independent organization throughout the war. At the time the OWM was created Byrnes relinquished the OES directorship and the post was filled by Fred M. Vinson of the District of Columbia Federal Circuit Court of Appeals. The OES and OWM subsequently maintained a cooperative relationship, partly because of the personal congeniality between Vinson and Byrnes.

The OWM and its successor, the Office of War Mobilization and Reconversion (OWMR) wrestled effectively with the universal problem of coordination in large administrative hierarchies. It is necessary to recognize that the need for top-level coordination is by no means evidence of poor organization. On the contrary, it is in major part "an index of the extent of specialization and the consequent division of labor,"[41] a division of labor that was dictated by the numerous economic sectors involved in the war effort. The proportions suggested by Eliot Janeway in which the domestic economy functioned in the war, "one-quarter coordinated and three-quarters uncoordinated,"[42] are highly debatable.

Postwar Planning: Reconversion

Establishment of the Office of War Mobilization and Reconversion in October 1944 was more in the nature of a conversion of OWM than a replacement of it. Byrnes added continuity by being appointed director of the new agency (he was succeeded by Vinson and more continuity in April 1945). OWMR was directed to assume OWM's responsibility to unify the parts of the administrative machinery; but there was added the duty of coordinating government planning for reconversion, specifically developing demobilization procedures, settling interagency controversies pertaining to the transition to a peacetime economy, relaxing emergency war controls, and consulting with state and local governments in reconversion matters. At the same time, OWMR was given jurisdiction over the Office of Contract Settlement, the Surplus Property Administration (successor to the Surplus War Property Administration), and the Retraining and Reemployment Administration.

The reasons for the birth of the new-name organization, this time a creation of Congress, not an Executive Order, stemmed from Congress' insistence upon a more influential role, especially vis-à-vis the executive, in directing the domestic war effort, plus its rising determination to reassert its authority in the already proliferating preparations for the transition. Congressional leaders concerned about that matter wished to avoid, like everyone else, the chaotic dismantling that followed World War I; and they were acutely cognizant of the ominous transitional potentialities coming out of a war that had committed a vastly greater part of the economy than had any previous conflict in U.S. history. An orderly transition therefore demanded careful advance preparations that would, among other things, try to reconcile rationally the inescapable jockeying for position among the conflicting interest groups. That attitude made it a bit ironic that the act setting up OWMR provided for an advisory board representing business, labor, and agriculture.

The reconversion impetus had surged in early 1943 as the military balance after the surrender of the German Sixth Army at Stalingrad in February clearly began to shift toward eventual Allied victory. Beginning in that year, and accelerating its efforts after the Normandy assault in June 1944, the OWM assumed a leading role in the effort to construct an integrated reconversion program; and indeed, its successor agency was faulted for excessive enthusiasm toward the relaxation of control.[43] Some indication of the wartime concern with the problem is apparent from the following selective list:

1943

Donald Nelson assigns Ernest Kanzler to make a study of, and report on, reconversion.

Numerous other studies of reconversion within WPB.

Establishment of Senate Special Committee on Postwar Economic Policy and Planning (followed some months later by establishment of a similar Committee in the House).

Establishment of the Baruch-Hancock unit within OWM (its *Report* in February 1944).[44]

Donald Nelson's Bureau of Planning and Statistics is assigned to study reconversion (its *Report* in January 1944).

Creation of War Contracts Price Adjustment Board under the Renegotiation Act of 1942.

President directs OWM to assume responsibility for planning postwar economic adjustment.

Truman Committee Report urges greater action on contract termination, surplus property disposal, and reconversion in general.

Establishment of Joint Contract Termination Board in OWM.

1944

President's annual Budget Message stresses importance of reconversion: "Demobilization begins long before hostilities end."

February report on cancellation of contracts, disposition of surplus property, and industrial demobilization and reconversion by Senate Special Committee on Post-War Economic Policy.

Establishment of Office of Contract Settlement.

Establishment of Surplus War Property Administration.

Establishment of Retraining and Reemployment Administration

Passage of Servicemen's Readjustment Act (G. I. Bill of Rights).

Issuance of Executive Orders of the President implementing reconversion recommendations of the Baruch-Hancock report.

Public release of Donald Nelson's reconversion plans, including famous "spot authorization" of production of certain civilian items.

High level of WPB Industry Division activity on reconversion, including programmed expansion of civilian production and preparation of a price ceiling formula for resumed production of consumer goods.[45]

Creation of the OWMR.

One of the astonishing facts about all this apprehensive preparation is how little influence it had at war's end in the achievement of what Senator O'Mahoney urged: "a series of terraces or stair-steps in letting industry down from the war peak to a peace level."[46] While it would be most extreme to say the 2½ years of reconversion preparations came to naught, the actuality was an all too precipitous dismantling, and

OWMR was one of the hurried termination advocates. Jack Peltason notes that "As early as September 1944, Krug [Julius A. Krug, chairman of WPB from September 1944 to December 1945] had adopted the policy of dropping as many controls as fast as possible after the defeat of Germany."[47] In fact, it was the official position of OWMR, revealed as late as its *Second Report* in April 1945, that large-scale reconversion should be postponed until the end of the war in Europe, that reconversion planning should remain essentially in the paper stage.[48] Of course, the Armed Services, bolstered by the German Ardennes offensive in December 1944 and pursuing throughout the cogent line that there could be no relaxation until both V-E and V-J, also quite successfully obstructed the reconversion effort. It was the decreases in military and rise in civilian output actually under way in late 1944 and in 1945 that cushioned the production transition. Otherwise, everything managed to happen rather suddenly after August 1945.[49] The disorder in the transition described a pattern, of course, and that pattern was again shaped by the interplay of conflicting interest factions. It was they, with an eager private market as handmaiden, who determined the parts of the prepared reconversion machinery that were to be permitted to function and the parts that were to be junked.

Dismantling the Apparatus

As for the career of the emergency administrative apparatus, it experienced, under the guiding hand of Bureau of the Budget recommendations, several kinds of demise at war's end. Some agencies or functions were simply terminated, such as the War Labor Board (December 1945),[50] the Controlled Materials Plan (September 1945), the Office of Price Administration (June 1946), and the OWMR (functionably terminated December 1946). The functions of some other agencies were consolidated and absorbed by established government departments. Such was the case with the War Food Administration in the Agriculture Department; the War Manpower Commission, which was carved up between the Labor Department and the Federal Security Agency in September 1945; the Reemployment and Retraining Administration, which also went to the Labor Department; some functions of the Foreign Economic Administration, which were taken over by the State Department; and the Smaller War Plants Corporation together with some functions of the Foreign Economic Administration, acquired by the Commerce Department. One prominent emergency control organization, the Office of Economic Stabilization, had its functions transferred in September 1945 to the OWMR.

The WPB, which had already terminated many of its subordinate units,[51] was assigned in November 1945 to the newly created, short-lived Civilian Production Administration, and the Surplus Property Administration to the newly created War Assets Administration. Final consolidation of the OWMR, the OPA, and the Civilian Production Administration took place when in December 1946 they were all brought together under the freshly established Office of Temporary Controls.

Perhaps it is desirable to try to unearth the core of effective agencies that were largely responsible for fashioning a workable body of economic controls. At the planning and operational levels below OEM, OES and OWM-OWMR, and aside from the commodity czar agencies, one would find about a dozen organizations. A plausible list of these would no doubt include:

1. The Armed Services.
2. The Maritime Commission and the War Shipping Administration.
3. The Foreign Economic Administration.
4. The cluster of labor agencies:
   Selective Service System.
   U.S. Employment Service.
   War Manpower Commission.
   Labor and Manpower Requirements Divisions of WPB.
   War Labor Board.
5. The Office of Price Administration.
6. The Industry and Commodity Divisions of the WPB.
7. The War Food Administration.

Even this brief list reveals the fact that World War II produced an economic controls bureaucracy of a magnitude never known before or since in the history of the country. Exclusive of military bodies, there were in all about 165 economic and noneconomic emergency war agencies. How atypical this interlude of administrative controls was in the American experience may be appreciated by the recognition that at the end of 1946 almost nothing was left of that apparatus. In August 1945 the President issued, and the public heeded, his stricture that private business should have every opportunity "to exercise its ingenuity and forcefulness in speeding the resumption of civilian production."[52] Nevertheless, the United States had not returned to pre-depression laissez-faire, nor had it seen the end to big government, for in the decades that followed the federal government's fiscal and regulatory role greatly expanded, and state and local government employment became an ever larger proportion of all jobs in the economy.

Chapter Five

Stabilization
and the Office of Price
Administration

ENABLING LEGISLATION FOR price control was the Emergency Price Control Act of January 30, 1942, soon implemented by OPA's issuance in April of the basic, legally enforceable, General Maximum Price Regulation (General Max). Prices of nonmilitary, nonfarm producers' and consumers' goods, rents, and initially the rationing of particular consumers' products, were matters delegated to this independent agency that had been created in August 1941—the lineal, pre–Pearl Harbor descendant of the Price Stabilization Division of the NDAC and OPACS.

As it was finally worked out with considerable administrative travail, the operational element in the rationing program was relegated to OPA by the WPB. The Division of Civilian Supply of WPB retained final authority to determine the commodities to be rationed, the amounts available for rationing, and the time for rationing.

While the OPA successfully constructed a national rationing organization beginning as early as January 1942 with the rationing of tires, the locus of rationing authority at the top level remained in a state of administrative disarray throughout most of the first year of war. For example, OPA administrator Leon Henderson, in an attack leveled particularly at the rash of new czar agencies established in 1942, declared at a WPB meeting as late as one year after Pearl Harbor:

the Executive Orders regarding Petroleum, etc., establish commodity organizations whose powers run counter to the functional organizations such as the War Department, the Navy Department, War Production Board and the Office of Price Administration . . . these orders are creating a serious administrative problem. The Office of Price Administration now receives directives on oil from Mr. Ickes, on food from Mr. Wickard, on rubber from Mr. Jeffers, on general rationing matters from Mr. Byrnes, and on other matters from the War Production Board. All of these agencies have the right to tell the Office of Price Administration when to start rationing. In addition, the Secretary of Agriculture is empowered to determine the conditions of rationing.[1]

Henderson concluded his remarks by bemoaning the incapacity of his local rationing boards to time the execution of new rationing programs. Despite Henderson's complaints about discretion over rationing, which probably any top official in the midst of such administrative clutter would have registered, the operational record of OPA with respect to rationing from the very first quarter of 1942, and from the end of the first quarter of 1943 with respect to prices, was impressively good.

There were at least three reasons for the effective rationing performance. One was that Henderson's organization finally accommodated itself to its status as a kind of service agency to the supply agencies: its function was to ration on request.[2] The second reason was the administrative exploitation of patriotism, community spirit, and integrity by almost 6,000 local, largely volunteer, boards.[3] As one leading analyst of the wartime rationing experience has concluded:

This basic rationing delegation to local, volunteer, representative boards was . . . a wise one. The unfamiliar, restrictive controls of rationing were much more palatable when local, unpaid citizens stood between them and the community than would have been the case if the controls had been applied by paid officers of the federal government—by "bureaucrats" . . . The sins of the local boards were never a strong club with which to bludgeon OPA, because the local boards represented the great American ideal of self-government.

It is doubtful, furthermore, that any other type of organization could have been set up within the very short time permitted by the emergency of war . . .[4]

The third reason for the success of rationing was the ultimately good coordination, in spite of much continuing distrust of the local boards, between community participants and the OPA salaried staff.[5]

OPA's effort in the vital price stabilization field during 1942 makes a far different story than the administration of rationing. Beginning in 1941 the price level was quick to express the mounting inflationary pressures, actual and expectational, from cyclical expansion, British procurement, the farm bloc, and the commencement of the U.S. military buildup. Here is the price record on an annual basis (1947– 49 average = 100):[6]

	Wholesale, all commodities other than farm products and foods	Wholesale, farm products	Consumer prices
1940	59.4	37.8	59.9
1941	63.7	46.0	62.9
1942	68.3	59.2	69.7
1943	69.3	68.5	74.0
1944	70.4	68.9	75.2
1945	71.3	71.6	76.9

It will be seen that the attempts at control did not produce evidence of stabilization until 1943–45, and for those years the indexes show remarkable stability in view of the powerful inflationary forces at work. Before 1943 the failure, especially in high places, of the price control authority to anticipate first the inevitability of American involvement, and then the need to build a control apparatus that drew upon local human capabilities, permitted substantial inflation to occur. Inflation is always a kind of jungle warfare. As the Bureau of the Budget history states:

The big farm organizations opposed control of farm prices; labor resisted wage controls in the face of rising profits and living costs; and manufacturers were alarmed by the prospects of heavier taxes.[7]

Manufacturers also feared rising money wage rates and desired to exploit the opportunity to profiteer by marking up prices on a rising income trend. Furthermore, the *expectation* of price increases and shortages in 1941 brought on to some extent precisely the results expected. These "get there first" attitudes intensified through 1942, and in the case of farm products into 1943, even as the OPA was bunglingly attempting to set up its price control machinery following the somewhat belated issuance of General Max.

Holding down prices was unquestionably one of the three outstanding administrative achievements of the war.

But price control in 1942 was a near fiasco, not only because of upward wholesale and consumer price pressures from the private market, especially stimulated by the explosion of government demand. It was a fiasco also because of blundering price control administration. The excellent record of OPA from 1943 on should not encourage historians to overlook the seeds of future trouble sown by the unnecessary consumer price increases during the first year or more of OPA responsibility.

In John Kenneth Galbraith's otherwise fine treatment of World War II price control,[8] the legitimately limited comments on enforcement effectively obliterate, as do almost all studies, the enforcement confusion and bungling in the OPA national office in 1942. Galbraith says, "it was realized from the outset that price control would require active enforcement."[9] He acknowledges that "in the early years of World War II, there was much anticipatory buying," then adds the sanguine judgment that, since high prices rather than shortages dominated business' recollections of World War I, "One might guess, therefore, that price control, as a restraint on anticipatory buying, was more effective in 1940–1942 than it would likely be in the future . . ."[10]

Of course, one can always assert that a policy is effective because in its absence things would have been worse. The presumption here, however, is that OPA enforcement policy was poor in 1942, even though after April it was armed with General Max and Galbraith believes that after April prices were "largely stable."[11] The immediate reason for this dereliction has been insightfully advanced in a neglected monograph by Imogene H. Putnam, one of the Historical Reports on War Administration.[2]

Although OPA constructed a far-flung and effective local volunteer field organization for rationing early in 1942, it failed to envision an active immediate role for such community participation with respect to price control enforcement. Nor did it sense the threat to the price control program from public indifference[13]—especially an indifference reinforced by OPA hostility to grass-roots initiative. Putnam perceptively uncovers the elitist source of the administrative blind spot in the OPA national leadership:

> A politician, a social worker, a psychologist, or an advertising man would have sensed the immediate necessity of gaining the firm support of the buying public; even the most brilliant lawyer, economist, or industry specialist might not. And price policy was at this time chiefly determined, both in its economic strategy and in its public relations, by lawyers, economists, and industry specialists.[14]

In *A Theory of Price Control*, Galbraith projects the well-known distinction between competitive and imperfectly competitive markets, and outlines seller/buyer behavior in the two types of situation. He then declares that "in the competitive market there is little hope that the buyer will police the price regulations imposed on the sellers; in the imperfect market . . . . there is considerable chance that he will."[15] Had Galbraith and his staff been of a different mental set, then if they believed that retail markets were mainly competitive, they might well have enlisted patriotic community participation to offset the presumed indifference and underhandedness of buyers.[16] If they thought such markets were largely imperfect, then they might well have presumed that with a little education on the matter housewives and other consumers could be a good source of supply for dedicated, community-conscious enforcement workers.

OPA top policymakers ignored for over a year three highly relevant documents at their disposal: a report on the effectiveness of the Canadian Price Control Law, under which volunteer housewives were coopted to exercise surveillance over retail prices; a report on how volunteer housewives in over one thousand U.S. cities in World War

I reported weekly on prices; and most portentously important, a detailed plan by consultant John H. Sly of Princeton University for the creation of grass-roots, unified Price Control and Rationing Boards.[17]

Under Sly's proposal, which in essentials and with the appropriate organizational divisions was finally embraced by OPA in 1943, the joint field unit would have a local volunteer chairman, volunteer price panels, and rationing panels of board members; volunteer price and rationing "wardens" attached to the panels who would, along with board members, maintain liaison with business and the community at large; clerical aides; and a paid district supervisor and trainer of the local staff.[18]

Unfortunately, the OPA Policy Committee adopted and proceeded with all due sluggishness to explore an alternative plan according to which price checking would be done by "professional shoppers"; any "self-appointed price policeman" would be identified as "fifth wheels and trouble makers."[19] The national office publicized this plan in brochures and press releases, while at the same time explicitly rejecting the successful Canadian system and warning housewives not to be "personal policemen" (sic).[20] This publicity, together with three vague letters mentioning price compliance, constituted the only national office communication on price to the local boards for nearly a year, during which time the Price Division under the Canadian-born Galbraith failed to recommend either community sponsorship or the appointment of price members at the local Rationing Boards.[21]

Putnam summarizes the gripping drama of the 1942 field organization deadlock:

Several months were spent on elaborate plans, ultimately abandoned, for a gigantic registration of all retailers by boards . . . The local boards did not so much reject General Max; they ignored it.

Not only the boards but the communities around the boards failed to become acquainted with the GMPR . . . A few inveterate consumers, noting prices higher than those of March, sent complaints to the ration board . . . There is no record they were ever answered . . . Volunteers offering themselves at the boards were absorbed at once by rationing. And they explained rationing to the neighbors. But what was Price? Who knew about General Max? Not the volunteer. And not the neighbors . . .

In June the Price Department announced a national survey of retail outlets, "mainly for educational purposes." The question immediately arose: who was to visit the Nation's two million retail outlets? . . . Kenneth Galbraith, Deputy Administrator for Price, talked of eight to ten thousand paid inspectors and publicly promised the retailers that "no Gestapo of volunteer housewives" would be used for the survey . . . But Congress, no fonder of paid inspectors than it was of volunteer snoopers, made a deep slash in the OPA budget, and "thousands of paid inspectors" were automatically eliminated from the argument.[22]

The fiscal blow in June and widespread violations of General Max inaugurated the turnabout. Price volunteers suddenly became acceptable to the OPA Deputy for General Services, but for another eight months the Price Division, engaged for a good part of that time in an intra-agency controversy with the Legal Division on the matter, failed to offer a program to the field offices.[23] As a result of the whole sordid history, when the Sly plan was finally put into effect, recruitment and retention of the volunteer staff was the major headache of the local boards' vital program for the next two years.[24] However, when the volunteer administration of price control was finally instituted in 1943, there can be little doubt of its success. The system was absolutely decisive for the maintenance of stable prices from 1943 to early 1946.

Under the Emergency Price Control Act no price might be fixed "with respect to any agricultural commodities without the prior approval of the Secretary of Agriculture."[25] Farm prices could not be altered unless they exceeded 100 percent of parity. Hence there was immediately created the problem of reconciling the efforts of an emergency agency with a broad public interest and the goals of an established federal department having a vested interest in the farm constituency. Indeed, that constituency extended much beyond the farmer: for example, the war brought with it a greatly increased influence by the processors of agricultural products.[26] In later years economists would employ the augmented term "agribusiness."

The President repeatedly called for resolution of the conflict between rising food costs, the cost of living, and wages. The average retail price of the Bureau of Agricultural Economics' typical "market basket" of foods rose from $347 a year in 1941 to $407 in 1942 and $458 in 1943—a 32 percent increase.[27] This sharp upward movement was arrested mainly by a "roll-back subsidy program," i.e., the institution of special federal subsidies to farmers and even heavier payments to processors.[28] It is noteworthy that OPA favored "stabilization subsidies" to get more output without disturbing consumer prices.[29]

In another major category of consumer expenditures, clothing, the price control record was even worse than it was for food; and it was worse by far after General Max. The apparel price index, on the same base as the earlier price index, rose as follows (1947–49 = 100):[30]

1940	53.2
1941	55.6
1942	64.9
1943	67.8
1944	72.6
1945	76.3

This index rises 17.6 percent from 1942 to 1945, whereas the consumer food price index increased only 12.4 percent, and the total index 10.3 percent over the same period. It appears that the major single reason for the excessive rise in both textile and apparel prices was the discontinuance by clothing manufacturers of many low-price lines.[31] The apparel price control programs, lacking the power and the necessary help from the WPB to command production increases in short lines, and under bitter attack by the industry and Congress, was "the weakest part of the whole governmental stabilization program,"[32] and remained close to that status throughout the war. But the failure could in all fairness not be attributed to any lack of tenacity or integrity on the part of the OPA.

The Price Control Act also permitted no direct controls over wages by OPA. Hence, unless common action with the other pertinent control agencies could be effected by OPA, these big administrative limitations and exclusions were certain to deprive the Price Administration of some of its virility, just as did the retention by WPB of the rationing initiative. On top of all this, the authority to issue actual food rationing orders, as noted previously in Leon Henderson's lament in December 1942, was in an administrative fog: although it was initially assigned to OPA, the Agriculture Department persistently intruded into the rationing process, and actual authority remained in limbo until February 1943 when that department was formally given the power to determine the need for rationing of food, its timing and extent, and the initiation of rationing differentials among various classes of consumers.[33]

The disengagement between OPA and wage control was especially ironic because General Max gave OPA authority to set price ceilings on all products affecting the cost of living. Wage control, in addition to "final determination" of threatening labor-management disputes, was the province of OEM's War Labor Board. However, the board initially could take up only wage issues growing out of industrial disputes that the U.S. Labor Department's Conciliation Service referred to it. This restriction for a time left voluntary wage settlements, preferred by organized labor,[34] outside anyone's administrative purview. Administration of both the limited wage stabilization provisions of the Emergency Price Control Act and the President's April 1942 message to Congress projecting a seven-point program to contain the potential upward spiral in the cost of living, were assigned to the WLB. The board's famous subsequent announcement in July of a formula holding wage increases to 15 percent above the January 1941 level in the Little Steel case (the "Little Steel Formula") was an implementation of these two price-stabilizing, regulatory actions. So likewise in purpose was the Congress' October 1942 Revenue Act, which drastically lowered personal income tax exemptions and raised rates.

But this was not all. The cost of living rise during 1942 was spurred in part by rising food and clothing prices and rising unmediated farm wages, with the attendant potential threat by industrial labor that it would demand higher wages. This ominous trend prompted a presidential Labor Day message to Congress under its Stabilization Act of October 2, calling for a new control agency empowered, among other things, to extend WLB's ability to prohibit *any* wage or salary increases without its approval—in the case of salaries, joint approval with the Bureau of Internal Revenue. Wage increases above the September 15, 1942 level were promptly forbidden. The WLB's wage authority, if not its capacity to actually enforce wage stabilization, was now completed for the duration.

The new permanent wartime control agency was a major step toward administrative integration because at the least it gave official expression to the close economic connection between wages, farm and nonfarm prices, the cost of living, profits, rationing, subsidies, and civilian purchasing power. The Office of Economic Stabilization, created in October 1942 under the directorship of James F. Byrnes, was further commissioned to work toward the resolution of disputes between control agencies, and in particular, in the price control field to foster cooperation between the OPA and the parity-conscious Department of Agriculture.

These crucial developments in the price field provided a striking example of unidirectional action toward a single goal, mounted within a framework of administrative fragmentation. The OPA, WLB, the President and Congress, the OES, and even the Department of Agriculture were all involved in bringing about what was one of the war's outstanding achievements in de facto interagency coordination.

Hugh Rockoff, among others, has examined carefully the conflicting claims regarding the effectiveness of price controls, as represented by the price indexes, from 1942 to 1945.[35] He cites Galbraith on the pro side to the effect that,

a myth to the contrary, assidously cultivated by devout friends of the market, these controls were highly effective . . . From 1943, when ceilings became applicable to food, the wholesale index was wholly stable . . . the Consumer Price Index increased between 1943 and 1945 from 51.8 to 53.9.[36]

Friedman and Schwartz, on the other hand, argue that

prices, in any economically meaningful sense rose by decidedly more than the "price index" during the period of price control, the jump in the price index on the elimination of price control in 1946 . . . reflected largely the unveiling of price increases that had occurred earlier.[37]

However, Friedman and Schwartz do concede that "it seems unlikely . . . that allowances for these defects [in the indexes] would reverse the qualitative conclusion that prices rose more slowly during the war than before or after."[38]

The concession appears to be considerable, for if *wholesale* prices during the 45 months from November 1941 through August 1945 had risen to an upper bound no more than the 23.6 percent that they officially rose over only 27 prewar months from August 1939 through November 1941,[39] then the wartime performance would still have been surprisingly good—about 6 percent a year compounded. For the first of these two periods, the actual BLS index (1967 = 100) increased only 14.3 percent. In only 19 months of U.S. participation in World War I, the BLS wholesale price index rose 19.4 percent. Rockoff concludes, with respect to the consumer price index, that there was a downward bias of between 4.1 and 6.8 percent as of December 1942.[40] The Bureau of Labor Statistics also estimated that there was a downward bias, of no more than 3.8 percent in that index for the period between January 1941 and September 1944.[41]

This record is all the more remarkable when one notes that the money stock, a major element in the burgeoning civilian demand and the inflation potential, had surged upward from $52.8 billion in April 1940, two years before General Max was adopted, to $67.4 billion at the time of its adoption, a 28 percent rise.[42] Between 1940 and 1944, the total production of nonwar goods and services fell from $180 billion (1950 prices) to $164 billion, while the money stock (December 1940 to December 1944) almost doubled.[43]

Appraisal of the effectiveness of the price control record, as Friedman and Schwartz point out, also requires reference to the course of price events when the war ended (see chart 5.1). They argue that general controls can only *temporarily* suppress inflationary forces, and that therefore the appearance of price stability is spurious: with the removal of controls the accumulated pressures will be released and prices will explode. The conclusion from this argument is that World War II controls were, like any such interference with the private market system, a failure in the long run, provided inflationary forces exist, as they certainly did at that time.

As previously indicated, the record shows that prices remained remarkably steady so long as price and wage controls were seriously applied, that is, into early 1946. But as political opposition to controls mounted, arguing that supply would "soon" catch up with admittedly excess demand, illegal price raising and relaxation of the law and its enforcement gathered momentum. The slow upward creep of the wholesale price index over the first half of 1946 was broken in July, after the suspension of price control in June, when that index (1967 = 100) jumped to 64.4 from the preceding month's 58.2. The lid was off. By December the index stood at 72.7, and one year later

Chart 5.1

SOURCE: U.S., Office of War Mobilization and Reconversion, *Report by the Director*, no. 8, *The Second Year of Peace* (Washington, D.C.: GPO, October 1, 1946), p. 17.

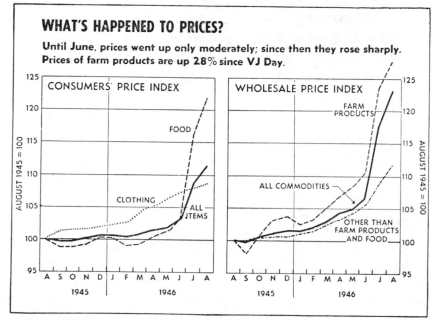

WHAT'S HAPPENED TO PRICES?

Until June, prices went up only moderately; since then they rose sharply. Prices of farm products are up 28% since VJ Day.

it had mounted to 81.4. The peak of that upsurge was in August 1948, with the index at 84.3. Thus, in the 26 months between June 1946 and the peak, the wholesale price index had risen 45 percent! As always, such a sharp price rise exacerbated immediate postwar social conflicts. Thereafter, prices fell off moderately, and it was two more years until they again approached the August 1948 level.[44]

It may plausibly be contended, therefore, that the supply catching-up process took a little more than two years. Such a process was also anticipated by those who in vain strove to retain firm price controls. They argued that a dangerous postwar inflation could be avoided with controls while civilian supply rose to meet pent-up demand. This issue was treated at the December 1951 annual meeting of the American Economic Association. Disputing Milton Friedman's statement that "controls apparently had little or no effect on the magnitude of full price rise" from the outbreak of war in September 1939 to August 1948, C. R. Whittlesey commented,

In early 1946 the controls were in effect and by 1948 most of them had been removed. Does the statement say anything more, then, than that direct price controls had no significant effect on prices when they were no longer in force? On the evidence of prices alone one might even infer that the controls were very effective and that it was a mistake to remove them when it was done.[45]

To resolve these two conflicting interpretations unfortunately would require examination of the counterfactual question, what would have been the rate and pattern of supply increase in the presence of continued general price and wage control?[46] Each of these two conflicting hypotheses no doubt implies a different answer to this counterfactual question. But the question has not been adequately researched, perhaps because of the great difficulties that would attend such an endeavor.

Customarily, money wage rate changes are often compared with price changes in order to get a somewhat more complete picture of a performance record, although the comparison is both simplistic and precarious so fas as drawing analytical conclusions is concerned. Economists have discovered no clear, invariant connection between changes in the two phenomena, especially when and if the connecting variable—labor productivity—is omitted from the analysis. However, the wage rate record for our purposes is of interest as such. Given that there is no meaningful average money wage rate for the whole economy, the manufacturing sector is probably the most appropriate proxy. Thus, we have average hourly earnings of "production workers" in manufacturing rising 55 percent between 1940 and 1945 (see below, table 7.4). It is noteworthy that the money wage figures, like those for prices, show a fairly steep rise until 1943, followed by a distinct slowdown after price and wage control, and the President's "hold the line" order on wages in April 1943, took hold. The same pattern obtains for real wage rates (i.e., the money wage rate divided by consumer prices). This is the feature of the wage record to be stressed here, rather than the direct and simple treacherous comparison with prices.

Chapter Six

Federal Fiscal
and Monetary Policy

IN A WAR economy, total money income, representing potential total demand, greatly exceeds the aggregate volume of civilian products as calculated at their prices immediately before the war. This excess, minus what would be saved, is a dangerous potential inflationary gap. It also threatens to create the popular illusion that more real civilian consumption and investment products can be gotten by letting the gap close through price rises. The harsh facts are that no more civilian products can be gotten than the physical volume produced, plus inventory drawdowns, if any, as allowed by the first-priority requirements of the military services.

To face these facts squarely, it would be eminently sensible for the government to tax away, or in some other manner sequester, all the excess money income. But people have always been reluctant to accept such an honest confrontation with sacrifices imposed by war; they or their governmental agencies therefore typically resort, through various policy manipulations, to a variety of piecemeal devices. John Maynard Keynes proposed in 1939–40 a plan for compulsory deferred pay to sop up some of the excess income, a proposal that later found supporters

Table 6.1
The Inflationary Gap in Real Consumption
(in billions of dollars)

	Real con- sumption	Personal money income	Pretax inflationary gap	Gap as percent of real consumption
1941	76.8	95.3	18.5	24.1%
1942	76.1	122.4	46.3	60.8
1943	80.4	150.7	70.3	87.4
1944	86.2	164.4	78.2	90.7
1945	93.1	169.8	76.7	82.4

SOURCES: Real consumption is calculated by applying the CPI index on a 1935–39 base (from the *Midyear Economic Report of the President*, July 1950, p. 135) to the standard personal consumption expenditure series. Personal income is from *Economic Report of the President*, January 1979, p. 208.

high up in the Roosevelt administration. The individual would retain title to such equitably extracted compulsory savings, rather than forfeit the funds as taxes, and they would be released to the owner after the war at rates appropriate to public stabilization policy.[1] But the main impact of this reasonable proposal, as in the case of a similar proposal in the United States, was merely to ease popular acceptance of the government's diverse taxing and borrowing demands.

In the United States, since, as has been noted, total real consumption changed but little between 1941 and 1944, almost all the war output came from the increase in the GNP and the drop in civilian capital formation, and that increase roughly represented the accumulating inflationary gap. National defense outlays totaled $304 billion from 1941 .through 1945. The vast size of that gap may be roughly and perhaps presumptuously[2] indicated by a comparison of actual real consumption, viewed as a proxy for consumption goods and services output, with personal income (see table 6.1). It will be noticed that the gap was not only very large, but it increased until the last year of the war. This is true even if we calculate in a similar way the gap after personal taxes, i.e., using disposable personal income (see table 6.2). The size of the gap was still huge, even though personal taxes took an increasing bite out of personal income—approaching by war's end the 1978 figure of 15 percent. It may also be noted for later reference that the tax-bite percentage more than doubled in 1943. In any case, much

Table 6.2
The Inflationary Gap in Disposable Income
(in billions of dollars)

	Disposable personal money income	Post-tax inflation- ary gap	Gap as percent of real consumption	Personal taxes as percent personal income
1941	92.0	15.2	19.8%	3.5%
1942	116.5	40.4	53.1	4.8
1943	132.9	52.5	65.3	11.8
1944	145.5	59.3	68.8	11.5
1945	149.0	55.9	60.0	12.2

SOURCE: Disposable income, personal income, and personal taxes are from *Economic Report of the President*, January 1979, p. 208. Post-tax inflationary gap equals disposable personal money income minus real consumption (from table 6.1). Personal taxes include all levels of income, estate, and gift taxes and personal property taxes, and exclude personal contributions for social insurance.

remained to be done to both finance the war and dampen the forces of inflation. Of course, we know that there was actual significant inflation before the effective operation of General Max price controls— for example, the 11 percent rise in the consumer price index in 1942 as compared with 1941. *Actual* inflation considerably reduced the nominal inflationary potential,[3] but the latter was still huge, which attests to the effectiveness of the general wage and price controls and rationing, the supportive attitude of the general public, and the efficiency of the other fiscal techniques used to siphon off excess money income and finance the military effort. The annual consumer price index rose only 10 percent between 1942 and 1945. Even if the index rise underestimated actual increases by 100 percent, the price control performance would have been remarkable, as argued in the preceding chapter.

Chart 6.1 shows roughly in what magnitudes, and implicitly in which proportions, the federal government drew upon taxes and bor-rowings to finance the war. It reveals that borrowings overwhelmingly dominated taxes as a source after 1941, but that tax receipts relative to borrowings jumped up sharply in the last two years of the war. Total budget deficits during the war years 1941–45 aggregated over $181 billion, and total budget receipts, mostly taxes, aggregated about $133 billion. One estimate has it that the Treasury was able to finance about

Chart 6.1
Sources of Federal Funds: Tax Receipts and Borrowings
Source: U.S., Bureau of the Budget, *The United States at War* (Washington, D.C.: GPO, 1946), p. 252.

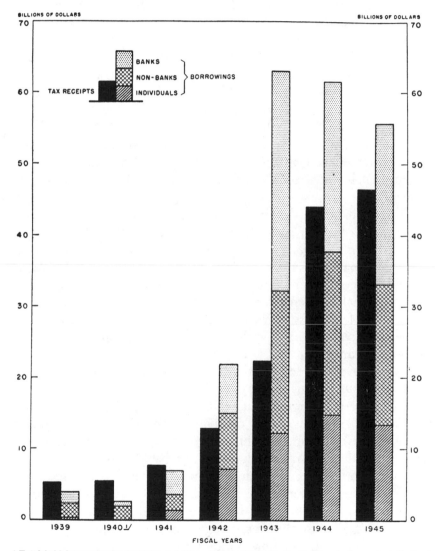

[1] Total held by non-banks includes .1 billion dollars which represents the net change in individual holdings.

Source: Bureau of the Budget.

45 percent of all war expenditures through taxation.[4] This is historically high, much higher than World War I or the Civil War.

As the deficits piled up, so did the debt. Under the New Deal it had doubled, standing at $43 billion on June 30, 1940, or about 43 percent of calendar 1940's GNP. At that time, 43 percent was historically large, exceeding even the bloated World War I ratio in 1919 of 31 percent of GNP. However, by June 30, 1946, the war had raised the debt over sixfold to $270 billion, or 129 percent of GNP that calendar year. While the post–World War II years were not, unlike the 1920s, years of absolute trend decline in the debt, they were nonetheless decades of decline of the debt in ratio to GNP until 1981. As early as 1955 the debt was down to about two-thirds of GNP; in 1965 it was 47 percent; in the next year the ratio had dropped to approximately the New Deal 1940 level; and in 1981 it was 34 percent.

There were several features of interest about the composition and ownership of the war-created debt. Individuals had contributed only about one-third in 1942, and proportionately much less thereafter, to the total of loan funds made available to the federal government. Also, in mid-1946 only 18 percent of the obligations were savings bonds— issues especially designed for widespread popular acquisition; and the great bulk of such issues were in denominations larger than $100. Hence, it would appear that the lower-income groups "did not own so large a share of the debt as might have been desired in the interest of a most favorable debt distribution."[5] Indeed, in the postwar era, while the public remained overwhelmingly the biggest holders, the relative importance of individuals, like that of commercial banks and nonbank investors (insurance companies, corporations, and mutual savings banks), in the ownership of federal securities was destined to decline greatly. It was the Federal Reserve banks, state and local governments, foreign accounts, and the new Social Security and other trust funds that accounted for the great relative increases in federal securities ownership from 1946 to the end of the 1970s.

Returning now to our pretax inflationary gap, summing to $290 billion, we may estimate how that excess income was "absorbed." We can roughly account for about $269 billion of it:

inflation took $84 billion, or 29 percent;

personal taxes took $67 billion, or 23 percent;

net increase in individual's holdings of government securities took
$49 billion, or only 17 percent;

the increase in individuals' nominal money stocks, M_2 (currency,
demand and time deposits), took $69 billion, or 24 percent.[6]

This accounts for 93 percent of the $290 billion. In other words, with respect to the "excess" personal income of individuals, taxes extracted only a modest proportion, and borrowing an even smaller proportion. (Low nominal, and even lower real, interest rates no doubt undermined individual desire to lend to the government.)[7] Actual price inflation, which among other aspects is always a tax on money balances, took proportionately more than either.

Individuals were still left holding large nominal money stock increases averaging over one-half their excess, potentially more inflationary, disposable income.[8] They were prompted to hoard, rather than spend, by commodity rationing, and by the sheer unavailability of many products. The division of personal household income as between consumption, price rise, saving, and income taxes is graphically shown in chart 6.2.

The aggregate (GNP) velocity of money consequently rose only slightly at first and then fell after 1942. The appropriate wartime monetary policy is strongly to constrain the money stock increase so as to impel the civilian community to maintain or increase the rate at which money turns over, i.e., its velocity.

The huge borrowings from the banks, shown in chart 6.1, indicate transactions that by and large added to the dangerously burgeoning money supply, rising 20 percent a year, whereas sales of savings bonds and notes to individuals, the smaller proportion, absorbed purchasing power. It is generally agreed that there was much too heavy a reliance upon borrowing from the banks because of precisely that money-creating, inflationary effect.

The Treasury, working jointly but not always harmoniously with the Federal Reserve system (Fed), contributed also to inflation of the money supply by insistence upon minimizing the cost of borrowing for war. Such an admittedly worthy, low-interest objective was probably

Chart 6.2
SOURCE: U.S., Office of War Mobilization and Reconversion, *First Report: Problems of Mobilization and Reconversion* (Washington, D.C.: GPO, January 1, 1945), p. 19.

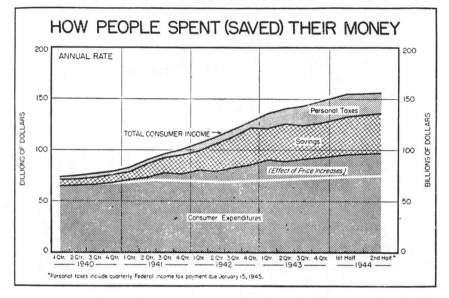

HOW PEOPLE SPENT (SAVED) THEIR MONEY

not weighed against the longer-term, and especially the immediate postwar, potential inflationary effects of rapid increases in the money stock in excess of the 20 percent a year that accompanied such an easy money policy. Indeed, the Treasury acted against the Fed's judgment in this respect, for the Fed authorities argued that low interest rates made it too easy for member banks to secure reserves.[9] In that situation, the Fed's perennial fear of inflation was most appropriate.

Also, because of price-pegging, government securities were like interest-bearing cash. This induced commercial banks to acquire them from nonbank investors.[10] Furthermore, by maintaining a wide spread between short and long-term governments, the Treasury stimulated member banks to unload the former on the Federal Reserve banks, thus augmenting bank reserves and, in consequence, the banks' deposit-creating powers. The Treasury also allowed member banks to pay for new issues of governments by giving the Treasury deposit credits (new money) that were exempt from their reserve requirements. U.S.

government deposits in all commercial banks exploded from $748 million in 1941 to over $24 billion in 1945, partly because of this easy arrangement for monetizing the federal debt. Aside from depriving the Federal Reserve of its powers of initiative in open market operations,[11] all this was hardly an anti-inflationary program. It therefore testified to the excellent price control record during the war, a record very close to that registered by Great Britain.

If the great bulk of personal income was received by the lower and middle income groups (e.g., about 80 percent of all family and individual income in 1941), individual income tax was potentially a powerful device for siphoning off a large part of the latent, inflationary excess of such income. In the context of Treasury rejection of a regressive general sales tax, collections by means of the personal income tax, pushed vigorously by the Roosevelt administration through reluctant Congresses, rose from 3.4 percent of all personal income in 1941 to a patriotic wartime peak of 12.2 percent in 1945. They had been only about 3 percent in 1929, but the wartime ratchet ended that laissez-faire proportion permanently; there was no returning. The percentage after the war remained high, and was about 11 percent in the 1970s.

The wartime feat was accomplished chiefly by regressively lowering personal exemptions, e.g., from the already reduced $2,000 in 1940 to $1,200 in 1942 for a married person with no dependents, blanketing new millions under the tax system in the Revenue Act of October 1942; by cutting in half the level of the first bracket of income subject to tax (1941); by steep increases in effective rates in all income brackets; by inaugurating a victory tax in 1942 on personal net income; and by instituting the withholding system, mostly on wages and salaries, in the Revenue Act of June 1943. The ratchet effect again operated after the war, with lowered exemptions, raised rates, and withholding continuing to characterize the federal individual income tax system.

The increases in the individual income tax collections, however insufficient to close the inflationary gap, struck like cyclones in each wartime fiscal year—from $1.4 billion in 1941 to $3.3 billion in 1942, twice that in 1943, $18 billion in 1944 and $19 billion in 1945. Such increases stimulated strong congressional resistance. Many members of Congress were not only obsessed with the presumed limits of taxable capacity but also believed that people should be allowed to build up savings during the war to provide a cushion against a possible return to depression conditions after the war.

Corporate business also came in for a substantial share of the tax levies. In addition to increases in the rates of the ordinary corporate income tax, surtaxes were added in 1941 and raised in 1942, and the prewar excess profits tax rates were continuously increased until the repeal of the tax after 1945. As a result, collections from all such corporation income taxes jumped from about $2 billion in fiscal 1941 to $4.7 billion the next year, twice that in 1943, almost $15 billion in 1944, and $16 billion in 1945. Collections from the excess profits tax exceeded those from the normal corporate income tax in every year from calendar 1942 through 1945.

Table 6.3 gives a quick view of the relative importance of the major wartime federal taxes, with a comparison for 1929 and two widely separated postwar years. In the peacetime New Deal fiscal year ending in June 1940 all federal tax collections were twice as high in ratio to national income as they had been in laissez-faire 1929. State and local taxes (revenues from own sources not included in the table), which followed a pattern of long-run upward relative growth, in ratio to national income were about 40 percent higher than they had been in the late twenties. But the proportion dropped to only about 9 percent of national income in 1942, and there was not much change during the remainder of the war.

The federal collections pattern within the total had shifted sharply between 1929 and the eve of the war in 1940. Repeal of Prohibition in 1933 greatly augmented the total for alcohol and tobacco excises, and the upward jump in that percentage of course reduced the relative importance of both types of income tax as of 1940. The introduction of the new employment taxes under Social Security created a similar effect. Thus the relative rise of excises and employment taxes considerably increased, other things being equal, the comparative regressivity of the federal tax structure. The two types of income tax together were only half as important in ratio to total collections as they had been in 1929.

But the wartime shifts in the structure of collections drastically changed the internal relationships. As total collections exploded to almost a fourth of national income in the last year of the war, income

Table 6.3
Percentage Share of Four Major Taxes in Total Internal Revenue Collections
and
Total Internal Revenue Collections as Percent of National Income,
World War II and Selected Comparative Fiscal Years

Fiscal year	Individual income taxes	Corporation income taxes	Employment taxes	Alcohol and tobacco taxes	Four taxes as percent of total collections	All collections as percent of national income[a]
1929	37.3%	42.1%	—	15.2%	94.6%	3.5%
1940	18.4	21.5	15.6	23.1	78.6	7.1
1941	19.2	27.9	12.6	20.6	80.3	8.1
1942	25.0	36.4	9.1	14.0	84.5	10.9
1943	29.6	43.2	6.7	10.5	90.0	14.7
1944	45.5	36.8	4.3	6.5	93.1	22.9
1945	43.5	36.6	4.1	7.4	91.6	24.2
1946	46.0	30.9	4.2	9.1	90.2	22.7
1950	44.0	27.9	6.8	9.1	87.8	17.4
1977	52.2	16.8	24.0	2.2	95.2	24.9
1982	55.8	10.4	26.7	1.3	94.2	25.8

[a] National income year is average of two calendar years, the last of which is the fiscal year shown in the table; e.g., the income year related to fiscal 1940 is the average national income for 1939 and 1940.

SOURCES: Federal tax collections are from *Historical Statistics*, pt. 2, p. 1107, ser. Y-358–365; *Statistical Abstract*, 1978, p. 268, no. 434, and 1984, p. 326, no. 521. National income is from the *Economic Report of the President*, February 1984, p. 242, table B-19.

taxes burgeoned. Consequently, while rising absolutely, employment taxes and the two excises dropped drastically as a share of total collections.

One of the most striking wartime changes in the collection structure shown in table 6.3 is the shifting role of the two types of income tax. Corporation income taxes, unlike the rising individual income tax proportion, ascend to a peak in 1943, then fall proportionately as peace comes. As it turned out, the relative decline after that fiscal year was the beginning of a long-run downward trend in the share of corporation income taxes in total federal collections. In the late 1970s, it was still falling, with the level of the share far below the figures on the eve of World War II.

In contrast, the share of the individual income tax, which had been substantially less than that for the corporation income tax in 1929, 1940, and well into the war, jumped very sharply in fiscal 1944, and, as has been noted, maintained the tax's new position as leading single source of wartime collections. In the decades following, the individual income tax collections, now to a considerable degree impervious to evasion by virtue of the withholding system, continued to rise until they accounted for over one-half of all collections in the late 1970s. Even as a share of total personal income, the percentage in the "peacetime" seventies somewhat exceeded the wartime maximum. What the American people did not accept, or were not asked to accept, in war they came to accept in peace—after long habituation. That acceptance evolved in the context of a secular rise in state and local taxes as proportion of personal income. Nevertheless, it was the war that firmly established the individual income tax as the primary source of federal revenues.

Not so with the social security and other employment taxes. The enormous absolute and relative growth in those was a postwar phenomenon connected with the great extension of federal income security programs, the unfolding of the New Deal's incipient welfare state element in the mixed economy. With individual income and employment tax collections comprising three-fourths of total federal tax collections in the late seventies, the federal constituent of the mixed economy and its welfare component was clearly very firmly grounded in a tax system heavily emphasizing the taxation of wage and salary incomes.

Chapter Seven

Wartime Social Changes

IN A WORK on economic history that treats the major social changes occurring in wartime, at least two criteria of selection should be applied: they should have had a noteworthy national or regional impact at the time, and they should preferably although not necessarily have had some long-run effects. These criteria of selection suggest, with regard to World War II, discussion of population and labor force change, the activities and status of organized labor, the war-connected experience of black America, Japanese "relocation," and the postwar veterans' educational explosion.

The unique experiences of women in wartime society would also seem to be an appropriate topic, but, save for their role in the postwar "baby boom," to be discussed here under population change, the important, war-induced alterations in women's economic and social role did not basically reshape the trends in their status during the postwar years. For example, women's labor force participation rate, the war work notwithstanding, has shown a steady rise of about 12 percent per decade between 1940 and 1979.[1]

It appears proper, therefore, merely to note that women distinguished themselves in noncombat units of the military services, and otherwise shouldered numerous burdens specific to their current position in society. Those burdens included severance from, or loss through disability or death, of sons, husbands, and lovers; particular stresses in the family fabric due to migration shock; the exacerbation of parent-adolescent conflicts; living in segregated, cramped, and substandard housing; insufficient and inadequate child care centers; and usually the double weight of holding a job and managing a home. No doubt millions of the women who entered the labor force found the experience in one sense emancipating, however.

When the war was over, while millions of women left the labor force because they believed they should give up their job to a veteran, other millions were the unwilling victims of veterans' preference policies in employment. Still others remained in the job market but found themselves occupationally downgraded into the traditional female pursuits.

Population, Migration, and Labor Force

While war brought little deviation from the characteristic moderate rate of population growth — 5.9 percent for the half-decade 1940–45 compared with 6.4 percent for the period 1925–30—internal migration and expulsion from home and community was necessarily very great. The farm population, as noted, fell drastically through out-migration, by over six million or one-fifth, between 1940 and 1945. Chart 7.1 shows how the war period stands out compared to any quinquennium between the twenties and the sixties. Eleven million men and women left their homes to join the armed forces. The great migration wave regionally was to the Pacific Coast, particularly to California. Both the region and its largest state gained at a rate above their peacetime, greater-than-average pace, with the three Pacific Coast states increasing their populations by over 34 percent, California by over 37 percent, between 1940 and 1945. These five-year percentage gains may be compared with 47 and 66 percent, respectively, for the entire decade of the 1920s.[2] Of the net national interstate migration of about 3.5 million between April 1940 and November 1943, nearly 1.5 million was into California.[3] The wartime above-trend increases

Chart 7.1
SOURCE: U.S., Department of Agriculture, Economic Research Service, *U.S. Population Mobility and Distribution*, ERS-436 (Washington, D.C., December 1969), p. 33.

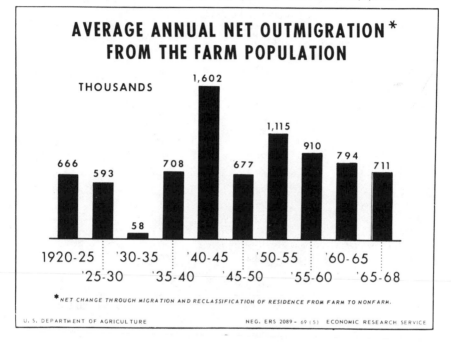

AVERAGE ANNUAL NET OUTMIGRATION*
FROM THE FARM POPULATION

THOUSANDS

* NET CHANGE THROUGH MIGRATION AND RECLASSIFICATION OF RESIDENCE FROM FARM TO NONFARM.

U. S. DEPARTMENT OF AGRICULTURE   NEG. ERS 2089- 69 (5)   ECONOMIC RESEARCH SERVICE

were primarily due to stepped-up net in-migration, responding to job opportunities in aircraft, shipbuilding, and other war-related activities.

Almost all other regions experienced either arrested population growth or losses, due mainly to out-migration. The exception was the big South Atlantic region, which gained population at a rate approximately on trend. The New England, Middle Atlantic, and East North Central regions containing the old manufacturing belt barely held their own during the war, but quickly regained their populations in 1946, thereafter continuing to exhibit their slow or U.S.-average growth trends.

The marriage rate has historically been long-run stable and cyclically sensitive, e.g., drifting upwards in economic expansion. Hence, the increase from 1939 to 1942, shown in table 7.1, should be expected in part because of that association.[4] But in addition, the 1941 and 1942 rises were no doubt induced also in part by the "war bride"

Table 7.1
Comparative Birth, Marriage, and Divorce Rates,
World War II and Selected Periods,
1920–1982
(rate per 1,000 population)

Period	Births	Marriages	Divorces
1925	25.1	10.3	1.5
1935	18.7	10.4	1.7
1939	18.8	10.7	1.9
1940	19.4	12.1	2.0
1941	20.3	12.7	2.2
1942	22.2	13.2	2.4
1943	22.7	11.7	2.6
1944	21.2	10.9	2.9
1945	20.4	12.2	3.5
1946	24.1	16.4	4.3
1947–51 average	25.0	11.7	2.8
1952–57 average	25.2	9.4	2.4
1958–60 average	24.1	8.5	2.2
1961–69 average	19.9	9.4	2.5
1970	18.4	10.6	3.5
1978	15.3	10.3	5.1
1982	16.0	10.8	5.1

Source: Data for computations, from *Historical Statistics*, pt. 1, pp. 49 and 64, ser. B-5, B-214, B-216; *Statistical Abstract*, 1979, p. 60, no. 80, and 1984, p. 63, no. 83.

psychology and the possibility of military deferment or draft postponement. Thereafter, the rate moved toward trend, represented by either 1925 or 1978. However, as the war wound down and terminated there was another jump, the excess over trend reflecting largely a combination of women leaving the labor force and men returning from military to civilian life. This produced the spectacularly high rate in 1946, together with a rate of almost 14 per thousand in 1947.

The divorce rate, on the other hand, in the long run has been rising rather than stable. It therefore seems likely that the high and rising rate during most of the war years was both responsive to high employment and approximately on trend. But again, as table 7.1 reveals, there was a great jump as the war ended, the rates for both 1945 and 1946 being far "ahead of their time." The reasons for this are not firmly established, but we do know that such a jump also occurred after World War I; some have argued that war marriages are unstable, and that divorces are postponed during the war so that they pyramid with its termination.[5] Also, hundreds of thousands of women gained a new material independence through employment during the war, and this fact may also have induced some of them to reject marital dependence.

The birth rate in the United States has exhibited a distinct secular decline: in 1900 it was 32.3 per thousand, and in 1978 it had fallen to 15.3 per thousand. The average rate for 1941–45 was 21.4 per thousand, no doubt reflecting both trend (being lower than 1925) and short-period, high-level economic activity (being higher than the depression years). But in addition, as a short-run phenomenon it reflected changes in the marriage rate with a brief lag, rising and then falling.[6] Again, the jump in 1946 no doubt expressed the optimism of war's end and the 1945 rise in the marriage rate. The birth rate for 1947 was 26.6 per thousand, the highest rate since 1921, one not to be equaled subsequently. The explanation must be the high 1945, and particularly the 1946, marriage rate, which was by far the highest rate recorded between 1920 and the end of the 1970s.

The Baby Boom

But perhaps even more interesting is the high countertrend average rates for the postwar decade 1947–57. This was the famous baby boom, and it occurred despite a concomitant clear drop in the aggregate marriage rate. But this drop in the overall marriage rate is deceptive: people in the *younger ages* in that decade were getting married and having children at a rate much above prewar 1940 and the war years, as well as above the rate after 1957.[7] Hence the U.S. population rose at a high 1.7 percent per year from 1946 to 1956 (as contrasted with 0.9 percent from 1966 to 1976.).

The baby boom, which raised the percentage of children in the population from 15.4 in 1945 to almost 20 in 1960, may be attributed in large part to the postponement of family formation during the war years. But high employment at rising incomes aided by veterans' benefits for young male workers also contributed.[8] Furthermore, as Rich-

ard Easterlin and others have pointed out, there was both a decline
in age at marriage after 1940 and a tendency for wives to have children
much sooner after marriage.[9] Easterlin argues that the baby boom
involved a coincidence of three forces: good income for young men
(demand factor), restricted immigration, and comparatively small
numbers of young entrants into the labor force (the latter two contributing to favorable incomes from the labor market supply side).[10] It
has also been hypothesized that the rise in the average number of
children under 18 living in the revitalized family setting in housing-
tract suburbia for a time appeased the yearning among adults for psychic
security in an age of increasing alienation within the adult world.[11]

The social effects of the ten-year, countertrend baby boom were
notable. One of the most striking was the great expansion in grade-
school, and later college, enrollments, with attendant explosions in
educational expenditures. While an important part of the latter was
due to both increased expenditures per capita of the school-age population and a rising proportion of the relevant population attending
educational institutions, a large part was undoubtedly because of the
relative growth of that population well into the early 1970s.

The impact of the baby boom on the age composition of the labor
force was also striking. By the late seventies (1979) the percentage of
young male workers (employed and unemployed) aged 16–24 in the
entire labor force was 13—a substantial increase over the 11.5 in
1960. That rise took place in spite of a sharp decrease in the proportion
of all males in the labor force over the same period. With respect to
women, while women of all ages became more active participants in
the money economy, those in the 16–24 year cohort increased even
more, so that by 1979 one in every nine persons in the total labor
force (11 percent) was a young woman. Participation by this female
cohort had grown so rapidly that by 1979 it was almost 87 percent as
large as its youthful male counterpart.[12]

The effect of the baby boom on lagged total labor force growth,
although unquestionably positive and large, is almost impossible to
determine with precision: too many other factors, such as the long-
run fall in male and long-run rise in female participation rates, influence the connection. In the short period, as Stanley Lebergott once
emphasized, "the essential and necessary relationship that links short-

run population and labor force change is simple to describe: there is none."[13] No sharp break in the growth of the labor force is detectable for the years when the babies reached 16 years of age. All we know is that the millions of persons 16 or older in the labor force as a percentage of the noninstitutional population, i.e., the participation rate, gradually drifted upwards from 58 in 1947 to over 63 in the late seventies. We can say that the male contingent 35 years of age or above after 1965 failed to grow absolutely, while the number of those under 35 increased substantially. The male labor force was younger. The same was not true of the women's contingent, in which all age groups specified by the Bureau of Labor Statistics up through 54 years of age showed substantial absolute increases.

It is even more difficult to speak confidently about the impact of the baby boom on either total consumption or, aside from infant and children's products, the composition of consumption. Clearly, family formation stimulated the demand for an important item like housing as well as for home-connected products. But the sustained housing boom of the fifties and the enormous increase in the number of owner-occupied homes can be attributed to the baby boom to only a minor extent. While the proportional rise in both the number of households and husband-wife families between 1947 and 1957 was unusually great, the high level of new housing construction in that decade was no doubt overwhelmingly due to the attrition of the nation's housing stock over the long, lean years from 1929 to 1945.

It is sometimes said that consumer product spending will be somewhat depressed as young adults choose children rather than such products. But it is more likely that the effects upon consumption were merely compositional, and there is no clear evidence on the aggregate level that either consumption or savings relative to income were affected.

Labor Activity and Organization

Overfull employment, worker patriotism, and public acknowledgment of labor's crucial role all conjoined to advance the social status of organized workers during the war. The jump in U.S. labor union membership from 8.7 million in 1940 to 14.3 five years later was a hallmark of that advance. Both the AFL and the CIO shared in the membership explosion. The former increased its numbers by about 63 percent, the latter by 66 percent over that five year period.

Unionists made up over a third of all nonfarm civilian employment by 1945—the historic peak proportion for the twentieth century. Thereafter the proportion held quite steady at about one-third until the late 1950s, when it began to drift downward to about one-fourth in the late seventies.

The rise of organized labor's numerical strength was in some ways a difficult experience for it, however. The atmosphere seemed reasonably favorable in the context of a year of militancy and growth preceding Pearl Harbor that greatly strengthened labor's industrial position. But setting up the National War Labor Board in January 1942 resolved neither long-standing conflicts with management over the closed or union shop, nor conflicts stemming from disunity in labor's ranks, nor the forthcoming difficulties facing labor in a wartime society that abjured interruptions in production.

Of the twelve-member WLB, its labor and public representatives by the summer of its first year had perforce adopted a so-called "maintenance of membership" (MOM) compromise between labor's minimal demand for the union shop and management's traditional insistence upon "workers' rights" not to join a union. Under MOM, workers had fifteen days to join and stay in, or not join. On the wage front the board, as mentioned in chapter 4, assumed the function of wage stabilization, and concomitantly rejected, in the interests of inflation control, the principle that wages should be automatically and fully adjusted upwards (indexed) with rises in the cost of living. The seeds of future trouble were thus planted in the spring of 1942.

In April the board approved a 4½ cent per hour wage rise in the International Harvester case despite a union demand for 12½ cents.[14] But a generalized decision was not hewed out until July, when in response to the United Steel Workers' demand for 12½ cents an hour in their negotiations with the "independent" steel corporations, the board approved only 5½ cents. This figure expressed the board's Little

Steel Formula. Labor was cajoled into acceptance of the Little Steel Formula partly by the promise of various fringe benefits.

The WLB recognized the labor ferment that the general application of the Little Steel Formula's money wage restraint was likely to create. It consequently inaugurated a quite pervasive policy of allowing industrial settlements that granted, in lieu of wage increases, a variety of nonwage concessions by employers as demanded by labor. These included such employee benefits as annual vacation and holiday pay, pensions, supplemental unemployment compensation, travel allowances, health insurance, and work-shift premiums. While the value of such supplements to money wages rose but moderately during the war, it mounted to a significant proportion of employee compensation as the postwar decades unfolded.

The notion of a productivity increment for labor was thus also rejected. It has been noted above that general price controls had not become effective by May 1942. The Board presumed otherwise. The consumer price index (1967 = 100), which stood at 48.7 in May 1942, had risen another 8 percent by May of the following year (who could know that the index would thereafter be stable until war's end?). And of course labor was prominent among the critics who averred that the index for several reasons understated the actual increase for wage earners, and also ignored quality deterioration.

The Little Steel Formula appeared to labor, given the continued upward price drift and the widespread agitation in government and "public" circles for a wage freeze, to be an unwarranted attack upon real wages. Violations of the no-strike pledge, which had from the outset been widely perpetrated, and not only over the wage issue, increased as 1942 waned. Labor resentment was also intensified in 1943 by the WMC's Order in April of that year freezing workers in essential activities to their jobs, thus blocking opportunities for possible higher pay elsewhere.[15] The number of workers involved in stoppages continued after 1942 to rise throughout the war and into 1946. The issue of wages (and hours) become even more prominent in the work stoppages through the year 1943.

The most bitter and tenacious struggle against the WLB was waged by FDR's now archenemy John L. Lewis and his United Mine Workers of

America, which had withdrawn the previous year from the CIO. As mentioned earlier, the bituminous coal strike raged, with the miners now out, now briefly back on the job, throughout most of 1943, inciting the government twice to take over the mines. At one point the President withdrew draft exemption for miners on strike who were under forty-five and subsequently, in January 1944, publicly reiterated his proposal for a national service law that would prevent strikes, require registration of all able-bodied adults, and make them available for government assignment by local draft boards to essential production anywhere. The pressure for a national service law, especially by the military, was a constantly recurring threat, particularly after the strike upsurge and severe labor shortages of 1943. But labor's fear of "involuntary servitude," business's fear of government controls, and liberal opposition killed the effort after the German defeat in the Battle of the Bulge.

One of the major issues in the miners' 1943 strike was labor's ground-breaking demand for "portal-to-portal" pay. Miners often spent as much as one and one-half hours a day on company property getting to and from the pit, and were not paid for this time. In the final agreement ending the strike this far-reaching principle of payment for portal-to-portal time was permanently accepted.[16]

The coal strike was most significant for other reasons. It demonstrated that organized labor would accept wage stabilization in an emergency only if the price controls were deemed effective.[17] Labor's historic fear than an incomes policy would most likely entail a wage but not a price freeze was again the theme of AFL-CIO head George Meany's criticism of President Jimmy Carter's wage-price guidelines in 1979.

The importance labor attached to the wage-price issue throughout the war years calls for a glance at actual developments—at least insofar as the official data may reflect those developments. Because of the prominence given to the mine workers' militancy it is appropriate to compare the miners' wages with those of the important manufacturing production workers. Table 7.2 shows a bit of the official evidence, and suggests that the average manufacturing production worker did not fare too poorly, at least until the last year of the war, considering the "war-sacrifice" setting.

Table 7.2
Comparative Wages of Bituminous Coal Miners and of All Manufacturing Production Workers, 1940–1945

	Average hourly wages in cents		Consumers price index	Manufacturing real wage		Miners' real wage	
Year	Manufacturing production workers	Bituminous coal miners	(1935–39 = 100)	Rate	Index	Rate	Index
1940	66	85	100.2	65.9	100.0	84.8	100.0
1941	73	96	105.2	69.4	105.3	91.3	107.7
1942	85	103	116.6	72.9	110.6	88.3	104.1
1943	96	110	123.7	77.6	117.8	88.9	104.8
1944	101	115	125.7	80.4	122.0	91.5	107.9
1945	102	120	128.6	79.3	120.3	93.3	110.0

SOURCES: Wage data from *Historical Statistics*, pt. 1, p. 169, ser. 802, and p. 170, ser. 813. Consumers' price index from *Economic Report of the President*, January 1953, p. 190, table B-24.

Indeed, during the years providing the immediate background for the 1943–45 strike upsurge, the official data show that manufacturing production workers were getting substantial hourly increases that in turn kept well ahead of the rise in the consumer price index.

Lewis, on the other hand, would seem to have had a point in his arguments that the miners were scarcely advancing in real terms, and moreover were losing relatively to "other workers." If the real wage rate index in table 7.2 for the bituminous coal miners is computed in ratio to that for manufacturing production workers and, expressed as a percentage, we get

1940	100.0%
1941	102.3
1942	94.1
1943	89.0
1944	88.4
1945	91.4

which shows a sharp and continuing relative drop for the miners until the last year of the war. Also throughout the war the miners' wages were well below prewar "parity" with their fellow workers in manufacturing. And the absolute level of their real wage rate after the post-depression 1941 rise was practically constant. The same was true of the real value of supplements to bituminous miners' wages (employers' contributions for pension, health insurance, etc.) until the last year of the war. Manufacturing workers' real supplements overtook the miners' absolute level of about $75 per year in 1942, and thereafter forged dramatically ahead.

The coal strike also reinforced the now well-established federal policy of presidential seizure of property in industrial disputes during "emergencies" or whenever the public welfare was deemed to be seriously threatened. There were 63 such seizures during World War II.[18]

Finally, historians generally agree that the coal strike stood out prominently in a year of rising strike actions as substantially responsible for passage of the War Labor Disputes Act (Smith-Connally Act), enacted over FDR's veto on June 25, 1943, "the first antilabor measure to pass Congress in a generation . . . "[19] Presidential seizure under the act was authorized wherever a dispute threatened interruption of war production; and any strike, lockout, or slowdown in seized plants was illegal, with violators subject to fine and imprisonment. Blackman records 66 presidential seizures under the Smith-Connally Act.[20] However, the law did not prohibit strikes called by a majority vote (as distinguished, so it was thought, from labor dictators), or strikes in plants not seized by the government. Nor did it seriously weaken trade unions or stop strikes, as the data on membership and stoppages indicate.

The Smith-Connally Act, interestingly enough, contained a clause forbidding unions to contribute to candidates for office in national elections (made permanent by the later Taft-Hartley law). This move was contributory not only to the historically growing trend of governmental intervention in the affairs of labor organizations, but also to an increased awareness of and desire to curb the heightened level of union, particularly CIO, political activity. The upheavals of depression and war, as well as congressional efforts to stifle union political activity, intensified labor's impulses to overcome its historic reluctance toward organizational participation in politics. The unions began to reject that tradition under the New Deal, for example in 1936 when AFL and CIO unions formed Labor's Non-partisan League. Despite many interunion conflicts over the matter, the unions moved away from political neutralism toward the use of the Democratic Party as the party of labor reform.[21] That viable liaison was greatly strengthened by the creation of a new Political Action Committee by the CIO in 1943.[22] Subsequently PAC played an extremely important role in the reelection of FDR for a third term in 1944.

In the months surrounding the war's end, the widespread efforts to assure a healthy postwar economy included a historically significant initiative by the Truman administration to plan for uninterrupted production through amicable relations in the nation's labor markets. In pursuance of this objective the President called together, after considerable preparation, representatives from the highest levels of corporate management and organized labor and instructed the Secretaries of Labor and Commerce to work with them. He also assigned a group of leading labor economists to serve as secretaries of the major committees created by the labor-management planning teams. The prestigious, four-week Labor-Management Conference of November–December 1945 expressed well the existing power relationships between business and labor; and the extent of both concurrence and disagreement at that conference anticipated some of the important legal and market developments soon to emerge in the sphere of industrial relations.

Three major issues absorbed the attention of the conference. The first was collective bargaining. The President had pronounced the conference theme of maintaining uninterrupted production. The assemblage implemented that theme with a historic concurrence by all sides on the principle of independent collective bargaining,[23] management's representatives strongly reflecting the views of the corporate-liberal Committee for Economic Development that had been founded in 1942.

But agreement on principle does not necessarily resolve specific major differences. Sharp and unresolved conflict developed on the conference's second major issue of "management prerogatives." Labor refused to accept any list of specific employer rights. In particular, it rejected management's demand that foremen, then organized into the strategic, independent Foremen's Association of America, be designated as managerial staff. Furthermore, employer spokesmen at the conference were insistent upon what they viewed as the *legal* responsibilities of unions under collective bargaining contracts. Labor, on the other hand, took the stand that the unions could and should assume sole responsibility for labor's adherence to such contract enforcement, abjuring judicial intervention.

As events unfolded, while labor adhered to this laissez-faire stand on contract enforcement responsibility, management, traditionally proclaiming opposition to greater government intervention in industrial relations, soon after the conference moved powerfully into the legislative arena at both federal and state levels to fortify its alleged prerogatives. The results of this employer movement included the Taft-Hartley Act of 1947, which, along with the notorious anticommunist "loyalty" affidavit and the exclusion of foremen and related personnel from protection by the National Labor Relations Board, made unions legally liable (suable) for strike-related damages that allegedly violated collective bargaining contracts. As noted earlier, and again below, the consequent "logic of history" was that public intervention in labor-management affairs was greatly extended and deepened.

The question of public intervention was also woven into the third major conference issue, in this case an issue involving the CIO on the one hand and the AFL together with the independent United Mine Workers on the other. In essence the former tended to rely to a considerable degree upon government help in dealing with the employers; the AFL and John L. Lewis of the UMW strongly favored "voluntarism" (market bargaining). Hence, the AFL's William Green, Lewis, and management's representatives all opposed CIO President Philip Murray's resolution favoring a general wage increase. This might seem surprising only if one were to ignore the aforementioned background presumptions of the labor opponents of the resolution: Green and Lewis believed, correctly as later events showed, that the CIO would invoke government aid (in this case in the form of "fact-finding" intervention in the steel and auto strikes) to try to get general wage increases in the big manufacturing industries. Their laissez-faire bias thus led them to oppose at the conference, despite rapidly rising consumer prices, a general wage increase.

The conference was also notable for one matter that it did not take up. That was the issue of communist influence in the labor unions. Neglect of the question can only be explained by the judgment that during the last months of 1945 the Cold War had not yet taken hold.

Black Wartime Experience

The *Negro Year Book* for 1947 noted four major changes affecting the lives of black Americans during the war: an increase of 600,000 black workers in manufacturing, the enrollment of almost 700,000 blacks in labor organizations, the induction of 1,150,000 blacks into the armed forces, and the migration of almost a million blacks from southern farms and rural communities to northern, southern, and western industrial centers.[24]

The war accelerated black migratory trends out of the South and from rural into urban life. The rural to urban shift accompanied the South to non-South migration and also characterized, as before, rural-urban migration within the South. Those extensive relocations brought significant occupational changes, and in their suddenness they exacerbated social tensions despite the professed antichauvinist aims of the war. Throughout the war the average American tried not too successfully to be anti-Japanese without chauvinism, anti-Nazi without antisemitism, and unbigoted toward U.S. blacks who were fellow patriots. Indeed the wartime racial crises and riots, by emphasizing the gap between American creed and practice, probably laid the basis for the civil rights movements of the fifties and sixties.[25]

Depiction of the size of the great migratory and occupational shifts is in some cases limited by a lack of intercensal data. However, what happened in these respects in the years 1946–49 (the census was taken in 1949) was so greatly determined by wartime experience that probably very little distortion results from using 1940–50 data.

The most distinctive decadal black out-migration in World War II, unlike the World War I decade, was the exodus from the South in general and Southern agriculture in particular. For farm operators, however, as distinguished from laborers, the downward trend in numbers that had begun in the South after the census of 1920 was arrested by the war; it was only in the last part of the war decade that the down trend was resumed. Indeed, the war prosperity in agriculture made possible a noteworthy, income-equalizing shift of black operators from tenants and part owners to full owners of farms.

Nevertheless, there was an exodus from the South and from Southern farming during the decade. While the Southern black population rose 17 percent in the United States, it rose only 3 percent in the South; and the percentage of blacks living in the South continued its long-term decline in that decade, marked by a sharp drop from 77 to 68 percent.[26] The proportion of all "nonwhites" residing in the non-South jumped 14 percent over the period 1940–50.[27]

It is true that the Southern urban black population increased by a million and a quarter, even as its rural population dropped by almost a million,[28] and in the United States as a whole the number of rural blacks, mostly all Southern, plummeted downward by 30 percent.[29]

But out-migration from the South was unquestionably substantial. The proportion of all nonwhites migrating between states, 14.1 percent from 1940 to 1947, customarily much *lower* than white proportions, was 45 percent *higher* than the latter in that seven-year span.[30] The great bulk of black interstate migration was a South to non-South movement. Four Southern states with large black populations—Alabama, Arkansas, Georgia, and Mississippi—experienced absolute declines in their average black male population over the decade 1940–50.[31] Long-run trends were reversed for the first time in three of those states. For seven important Southern states, the net out-migration of over half a million black males (female numbers closely approximated those for males) amounted to over a fifth of the total average male population of these states, 1940–50. On the other side, for five big non-Southern receiving states and the District of Columbia, the net in-migration of almost half a million black males added 46 percent to their total average male population for that decade. A quarter million black male and female in-migrants (net) were added during the war decade to California's 1940 black population of 124,000. Illinois had a black population of 387,000 in 1940 to which 180,000 black in-migrants were added in the ensuing decade.

By and large, and despite the hard, insecure, impoverished, and discriminatory conditions of ghetto life in the non-Southern cities, migration, in conjunction with severe labor shortages, brought material improvement. That is ordinarily what migration is all about. Writing on the contribution of migration to black betterment in the United States, John Kenneth Galbraith appropriately concludes,

Until World War II, the rural dwellers of the southern states were caught in a tight equilibrium of poverty . . . . the first efforts [of government] were, characteristically, devoted to facilitating escape within the equilibrium, to helping black sharecroppers become progressive farmers on their own. The equilibrium *was* eventually broken, but by people moving away. Before World War II, there were 1,466,701 black farm workers in the rural labor force of the old Confederacy, all, virtually without exception, exceedingly poor. In 1970, there were 115,303.[32]

With the exodus from rural poverty and tight industrial labor markets went major advancement in the occupational structure of black employment, South and non-South. Almost all those occupational shifts were on trend, however. War jobs merely accelerated the long-term evolution. For example, over a fifth of all black males were "farmers and farm managers" in April 1940, but only 14 percent were so engaged in April 1944.[33] The percentage was 5.5 in 1959 and 1.2 in 1971. About another one-fifth were farm laborers in April 1940, but these had declined to 14 percent in April 1944. Subsequent years brought further declines. Black industrial workers (craftsmen, foremen, and operatives), on the other hand, accounted for 17 percent of all black male employed persons in early 1940, but this proportion had jumped up to almost 30 percent four years later. Again, wartime economic exhilaration greatly speeded up trends that thereafter again raised the numbers to 40 percent by 1971. Only the large proportion of nonfarm male laborers—about another fifth—was unaffected, by either war or postwar conditions.

For black women the exodus from paid farm labor, which had engaged 13 percent of their total employed in April 1940, was so huge that four years later only about 5 percent were so engaged. As with the case of black men, women industrial "operatives" jumped up, from 6.3 percent of all employed females in April 1940 to 17.3 percent in April 1944, a proportion thereafter roughly sustained but not augmented. Over the same wartime period the percentage of black female domestic workers among all employed black women dropped sharply from 60 percent to about 45 percent, again an acceleration of a trend that carried the proportion downwards to 16.5 percent in 1971. Even higher percentages of black women entered service work other than private household, and the wartime jump was dramatic, from 10 to 18 percent, a ratio that continued to grow into the seventies.

Blacks made significant inroads into government, particularly federal employment, during the war, gains not only in numbers but also in occupational upgrading. Whereas black people accounted for about 10 percent of all federal civilian workers in 1938, they were 12 percent by 1944.[34] This may be compared with the 9.8 percent of all employed men who were black in April 1944.[35] Some indication of upgrading may be gleaned from a comparison of two studies, one in 1938 showing that 90 percent of all black federal workers in the District of Columbia were custodial, 9.5 percent clerical, administrative, and fiscal (CAF); the other in 1944, showing that for all federal departmental civilian black employment, 49 percent of the black contingent was CAF, 39.6 percent crafts-protective and custodial.[36] While the upgrading in departmental employment represented a lasting trend, the numerical advances were retained only at approximately 1944 levels after the war. These occupational gains in government civilian service were not mirrored to an equivalent degree in private industry, however, for an excessive proportion of wartime black manufacturing employment was in war industries such as shipbuilding, gun manufacture, and war-related iron and steel foundry products—low-level jobs in activities with a poor civilian future.

The suddenness of the wartime influx of blacks into these nontraditional urban occupations and areas was a shock to many illiberal whites, especially in the South, a shock that was intensified by the associated flood of new interracial social contracts against a background of intransigent segregation. The urban housing shortage and the spatial expansion of the ghetto magnified white segregationist and chauvinist attitudes. The concomitant interracial tension was further aggravated by a strengthened assertiveness and stepped-up activism on the part of blacks, stemming from their expanded urban job participation, their penetration into the trade unions, their million-strong contingent in the armed forces, and their determination to hold the whites to the professed antiracist and democratic goals of the war effort. Social struggle and conflict now superseded economic controversies in black-white adversary relationships.

The outcome was that the wartime employment and occupational advances were accompanied by very mixed short-run results with respect to the black struggle for social, educational, and political equality. In the long run, however, results on all fronts were undoubtedly improved by the often harrowing, sometimes deadly, experiences of blacks in the war period.

"What these foolish leaders of the colored race are seeking is at the bottom social equality" wrote Secretary of War Henry L. Stimson in his diary for January 24, 1942.[37] The War Department early in the conflict took the stand that it would not permit the military to serve as a laboratory for social experimentation.[38] The military's initial policies stipulated segregated units, no black superior in rank to a white in the same unit, white officers over enlisted blacks, segregation of black's blood plasma (with the Red Cross), segregated recreational, health, and eating facilities ("separate but equal"),[39] and widespread assignment of blacks to menial service duties (even some segregated black combat units). However, as the war proceeded, considerable integration gradually developed. Unfortunately, integration on the combat level was only brought into prominence in connection with the use of black volunteer troops in the desperate, bloody days of the Battle of the Bulge. Segregation in the armed forces ended officially only with an Executive Order by President Harry Truman on July 26, 1948.[40]

On the civilian front, furor ensued when the distinguished and militant A. Philip Randolph, president of the AFL-segregated Brotherhood of Sleeping Car Porters, threatened in the summer of 1941 to organize fifty to a hundred thousand people to march on Washington to demand equal employment opportunities for blacks in defense industries. It is generally conceded that FDR's famous June 25 Executive Order 8802 prohibiting job discrimination in such industries was both a response and a compromise to forestall Randolph's incipient movement. The march never came off. While the FEPC, somewhat strengthened by a new Executive Order in June 1943, did intervene successfully in a number of bitter conflicts, its appropriations and staff size were dwarfed by congressional opposition from both the South and the North, it could move only in response to a formal complaint, and it lacked significant enforcement powers. "Its ultimate weapon— requesting cancellation of a defense contract—was no weapon at all, for the administration was unwilling to jeopardize war production.[41] Nevertheless, there were a few exceptions, such as a Philadelphia transit strike, a so-called hate strike by white old-line unionists, in which threatened interruptions of the war effort worked out on the side of the blacks. Also, there were probably long-run salutary repercussions: in Charles E. Silberman's judgment Executive Order 8802 was "enormously significant: it represented the first time since Reconstruction that the Federal Government had intervened on behalf of Negro rights; and it demonstrated that Negro militancy could pay off. The seeds of the protest movements of the 1950s and 1960s were sown by the [threatened] March on Washington."[42] Although to establish the link involves speculation, the wartime FEPCs probably set the stage for future presidential executive orders on the same general matter in 1946, 1953, and most important, in 1961, the last named setting up the President's Committee on Equal Employment Opportunity. Coverage of these orders applied to firms doing business with the federal government—an expanding category. Also, between the war's end and passage of the Civil Rights Act of 1964, over half the states and many major cities had adopted FEPC-type laws and ordinances.[43]

The issue of discrimination during the war involved not merely employment but also training for jobs. As the war heated up, the growing shortages of skilled and semiskilled white males dictated steps to overcome the background of discrimination, in general, in vocational education, and in the vital matter of apprenticeship training as conducted by both employers and unions. Executive Order 8802 anticipated as early as June 1941 the coming needs and pressures when it stipulated that

All departments and agencies of the government of the United States concerned with vocational and training programs for defense production shall take special measures appropriate to assure that such programs are administered without discrimination . . .

That hopeful expression, however, encountered hard going throughout the war in all aspects of training—pre-employment, on-the-job, in the military, and apprenticeship. For example, in January 1942, out of 4,630 pre-employment and refresher training courses in the Southern states, only 194 were open to black trainees.[44]

The situation by the end of 1942 outside the South was rather better, despite an excessive but understandable concentration of pre-employment training for shipbuilding, aircraft, and machine shop jobs. In the country as a whole, the proportion of blacks among all pre-employment trainees rose from 5 to 10 percent between July 1941 and December 1942.[45] There was further progress in the next two years, including employment of black women as war workers.[46] By October 1944 a total of 324,000 blacks had received pre-employment and supplementary defense job training, and the South's share of such black trainees had substantially increased.[47] As for training and upgrading on the job, estimates are unavailable, but considerable activity can be inferred from the great relative growth of black male operatives, craftsmen, and foremen in industry from 8.8 percent of all men in depression 1940 to 13.7 percent in 1944 (a proportion that had edged up by only about one percentage point a decade later, but thereafter climbed steadily to 18 percent by 1965).[48]

In the armed forces, despite the heavy concentration of blacks in the service units, many thousands received training for new technical pursuits in the air corps, engineers, transportation corps, and coast and field artillery. Robert C. Weaver alleges that the Great Lakes Naval Training Center was undoubtedly "the most extensive and the best program of industrial education ever made available to Negroes in one installation.[49]

Of course, job results after the war were the acid test of the meaning of wartime training breakthroughs. The picture may be seen cursorily by a glance at the occupational distribution (percentage) of nonwhite employed men taken as a proportion of total male employment at two dates with respect to those occupations in which nonwhites represented either important or significantly unimportant shares:[50]

	1955	1965
professional and technical	2.7%	4.6%
clerical	6.3	7.9
blue-collar	11.0	11.9
craftsmen and foremen	3.9	5.6
operatives	10.7	12.4
nonfarm laborers	27.8	25.7
service	22.3	21.6
private household	47.6	29.8
other	21.9	21.5
farm laborers and foremen	20.9	24.4

These data show that the wartime training, which was directed largely toward work as craftsmen and operatives, did not eventuate in jobs that absorbed, by the midsixties, anything approaching the major contingent of black male workers. Even twenty years after the war's end, black men, who numbered 9.7 percent of all employed men, were heavily occupied in doing common labor and service work; and they were notably underrepresented in skilled labor, professional, technical, managerial, sales, and even clerical activities.

Japanese "Relocation"

One of the harshest episodes of the war within the country was the forcible uprooting of 110,000 Japanese, most of them Nisei or American citizens, from their homes, farms, and businesses on the West Coast. These evacuees were corralled into ten hastily constructed internment camps for the duration, from March 1942 to 1945. This forced relocation program was in a much later year termed "understandable" by U.S. Senator S. I. Hayakawa, who noted that "even the JACL [Japanese American Citizens League] supported it at that time."[51]

In addition to the personal anguish and outright violence suffered by those overwhelmingly loyal Americans, their property losses were enormous. Hasty evacuation prompted sales at distress prices, unreliable storage arrangements, pilferage, vandalism, and destruction by bigoted native patriots and competitors, and even the prosecution of escheatment actions by the State of California against a number of Japanese families who allegedly owned land in violation of the state's 1913 Alien Land laws.[52] The evacuation and internment destroyed the primarily agrarian economic base of the prewar Japanese communities of the West Coast, of a people who grew 90 percent of the area's strawberries, 73 percent of the celery, 70 percent of the lettuce, half the tomatoes, and most of a number of other important truck crops.[53] Of an estimated $200,000,000 worth of property possessed by the evacuees at the time of evacuation, the U.S. government, under its Evacuees Claims Act, paid in recompense only about $38,000,000.[54] As late as 1978 the Japanese American Citizens League by unanimous resolution sought from the government $25,000 redress for each Japanese-American sent to relocation camps, and the pressure for reparations, despite judicial discouragement, continued into the eighties.

The Veterans' Educational Explosion

One study of the Servicemen's Readjustment Act of June 22, 1944 ("GI Bill of Rights") concluded that "the fear of unemployed veterans, not the fear of maladjusted veterans motivated the persons who enacted the G. I. Bill."[55] Whatever humanistic or proveteran bias was at work, the social, political, and economic portent connected with demobilization was unquestionably as ominous as the lobbying American Legion alleged. The armed forces speedily dropped 8 million of their personnel from 1945 to 1946, and another 2 million by 1947. The number of World War II veterans in civilian life jumped 12 million over the same short two-year span.[56]

The flight of 2.6 million women, together with a substantial contingent of wartime civilian men, from the civilian labor force hardly could provide compensating job opportunities for such a vast influx. Fortunately, to the surprise of numerous pundits, postwar slump appleselling did not materialize, and total civilian employment jumped from about 53 million in 1945 to almost 58 million in 1947. But even if these openings were totaled (to 8 million), there would still be a considerable gap to be filled, a gap but little affected by the $300 mustering out pay given to those serving over sixty days and overseas in accordance with the Mustering-Out Pay Act of February 1944.

The World War II GI Bill contained provisions for a year of unemployment allowances at $20 per week, payments for enrollment in on-the-job or apprenticeship vocational and liberal arts education programs, special veterans' access to surplus war property, farm loans and home loans similar to those extended by the Federal Housing Administration under the National Housing Act of June 1934,[57] assistance in job creation and placement, and subsidies for rehabilitation of the disabled. There was no such program for the "veterans" of the merchant marine. The beneficiaries of veterans' unemployment allowances under the "52-20" provision of the GI Bill averaged about a million for 1946 and 1947,[58] and enrollment in all types of training and education programs absorbed most of the remaining demobilized excess labor. America had thus added an extensive new dimension to what one authoritative work has called the country's dual welfare system — one for the general population, one for the veteran population.[59]

Under an act allowing each veteran a $75 monthly allowance and up to $500 a year for tuition, fees, and books, it was the enrollment in institutions of higher education that had the most spectacular and long-lasting effects. About a million veterans were enrolled in such institutions from 1946 through 1948, constituting between 40 and 50 percent of their total enrollment, with 844,000 in 1949 and almost 600,000 in the first year of the Korean War as the World War II numbers gradually tapered off until the official termination of the act in 1956.[60] Of course the World War II GI Bill had set a veterans' education precedent possessing a momentum no longer derived from the short-run motivations that underlay the original bill. Consequently, the Korean War again raised the number of veterans enrolled in colleges and universities to a peak of almost a half million in 1956. Then the Vietnam War exploded, leading to the Veterans Readjustment Act of 1966, followed by another jump in veterans' enrollment that carried the total to almost two million by 1976.[61] But the World War II bill was the largest educational program by far. Of 15.6 million eligible veterans, fully one-half participated in education and training programs of all types, at a cost of $14.5 billion.[62]

The inundation of veterans enjoying the privilege of up to four years of college enrollment contributed immensely to the dissemination and democratization of higher education and the advance of technology in the United States. The innovative elitist Robert M. Hutchins, president of the University of Chicago, declared in December 1944 that under the GI Bill

Colleges and universities will find themselves converted into educational hobo jungles. And veterans, unable to get work and equally unable to resist putting pressure on the colleges and universities, will find themselves educational hobos . . . . education is not a device for coping with mass unemployment.[63]

But Hutchins was wrong. Despite overcrowding in housing and classrooms, disrupted learning facilities, and faculty shortages, the GIs performed better than average academically, and exhibited a superior seriousness about their studies. A *Fortune* magazine study of the class of 1949, 70 percent of whom were veterans, concluded that it was "the best, . . . the most mature, . . . the most responsible, . . . and the most self-disciplined group" of college students in history.[64] Furthermore, while the proportions of the nonveteran population that were entering the higher education sphere were also rising in the postwar era, the influx of veterans greatly contributed to a revolution in the spatial accessibility of the college and university. The establishment of scores of new campuses in urban environments finally broke the pastoral pattern of location inherited from a nineteenth-century bias against the city youth who had to live at home, work, and commute daily in order to attend college.

Civilian Welfare and the Level of Living

War brought a rise in the intensity of labor for thousands of workers. "Swing" and "graveyard" shifts (4:00 to midnight and midnight to 8:00 A.M.) and wearying overtime placed extraordinary burdens upon workers in the big war production centers. Hours of commutation to and from the workplace in those centers were, like work time itself, stretched out far beyond what was considered desirable in peacetime.

Many thousands of families were uprooted and internally disrupted. Newcomers often encountered hostility, racial and other, between themselves and the long-time residents of war-boom communities. People were frequently crowded into woefully insufficient and poorly maintained housing space. In the nation as a whole, even with the federal war housing program, the total net nonfarm housing stock declined. Expanded and federally subsidized child care facilities under the 1940 Lanham Act for families with the mother working were insufficient and often poorly staffed.

An unevenly distributed rationing program reflected and tried to manage fuel and food shortages in such items as gasoline and fuel oil, automobile tires, work shoes, meat products, edible fats and oils, and some processed foods like sugar and coffee. Rationing was inaugurated over the year 1942 in most cases, and, unlike the British system where some foods were still rationed in the early 1950s,[65] was terminated promptly in 1945.

There were large and real absolute decreases in total consumer expenditures between 1941 and 1945 on some items considered important in ordinary times. Prominent among these, in the durable goods category, were major home appliances, new cars and net purchases of used cars, furniture, and radio and TV sets. It makes a revealing comparison, in view of the petroleum conservation outcry some thirty years later, to note that real household expenditures (in 1972 dollars) for gas and oil plummeted from $5.4 billion in 1941 to only $2.7 billion in 1944, rising to only $3.5 billion in the following year. This was accomplished by limited availability through rationing, car pools, restrained recreational use of motor vehicles, added use of public transit, and a general public willingness to conserve. The compact car had not yet appeared.[66]

Advances in public education, which had been arrested in some respects by the depression, were further checked by the war. There was classroom overcrowding, high teacher turnover, a net exodus of teachers, lowering of standards, part-time attendance, high dropout rates in the high schools, and a slowdown in expenditure rates.[67] The number of working teenagers rose from 1 to 3 million between 1940 and 1944.[68] Expenditures in constant dollars per pupil in average daily attendance at public elementary and secondary schools, which had been gradually rising since a 1934 low, declined absolutely between 1940 and 1944.[69] A net total of over a million high school students left school between 1940–41 and 1943–44,[70] again reversing an enrollment rise that had been taking place through the depression years. In 1940, about 29 percent of the 18–19 year old population was enrolled in school, but in 1945 this percentage had dropped to about 21.[71] Even enrollment in federally aided trades-and-industry programs, after rising strongly between 1940 and 1942, as pointed out earlier, dropped steadily throughout the remaining years of the war.[72] In higher education, while about 280,000 were enrolled as trainees under the armed forces in a limited number of institutions in November 1943,[73] the number of civilian students in 1944–45 was only 54 percent of what it had been in 1939–40.[74] The issue of student deferment was not resolved until the beginning of 1944.[75]

There were other moderate sacrifices. For example, certain types of recreational activities experienced drastic curtailment, such as visitations to national parks, monuments, and forest lands, and to various state parks. The amount of leisure and recreational time also declined as people worked and commuted longer.

Yet in the four-year struggle for survival it is doubtful that the administrative weakness of the government's civilian supply agencies meant that civilian Americans suffered serious inroads upon their material level of living — especially in comparison with allies, many of whom experienced war's direct destruction in addition to much greater material deprivation with respect to the ordinary amenities of life. This is essentially the conclusion drawn in 1943 by Faith Williams, chief of the Cost of Living Division of the Bureau of Labor Statistics.[76]

The U.S. civilian experience as a whole must be appraised in the light of the fact that the resident civilian population declined from 131.6 million in 1941 to 126.7 million in 1944 (slightly higher in 1945, due to rapid demobilization).

It has already been noted that total personal consumption rose in real terms during the war, and when that aggregate is converted into per capita civilian figures, the rise is striking. In the case of food, for example, real annual civilian per capita food outlays rose from $560 in 1941 to $700 in 1945. Three of the four indexes of per capita food consumption in *Historical Statistics* show moderately rising wartime trends.[77] Fuel oil and coal, total expenditures for which held about steady over the period, clearly increased on a civilian per capita basis. This was equally true of the important clothing and shoes category. Outlays for medical care likewise rose, on both an aggregate and a per capita basis. Civilian health and medical care apparently fared about as usual during the war. The incidence of disease was not out of line with trends, with the notable exception of gonorrhea, which spread frighteningly from 147 per 100,000 of the population in 1941 to 226 in 1945, a rise that was not arrested until after the 1947 figure of 284.

The previously cited fall in the nation's net nonfarm housing stock needs to be reinterpreted. When viewed on a per capita basis, that decline was roughly proportionate to the fall in the resident civilian population. Hence, the civilian per capita stock was about the same at war's end as it had been in 1941. But the national burden of inadequate housing hit the American public more forcibly after demobilization. Already by 1947, for example, the resident civilian population had jumped about 12 percent above its 1944 nadir, whereas the real net value of the private housing stock had risen a much smaller 4.6 percent. however, a boom in housing construction (unfortunately peaking in 1950) contributed to some reduction in the gap.

While labor's added wartime burdens, particularly in the war-bloated communities, should be recognized, the fact of overfull employment of the civilian labor force would seem to be a major compensating benefit, especially after eleven years of depression. Aside from the psychic rewards that accompanied the elimination of unemployment and persistent job uncertainty for the employed, the rise in monetary rewards to American workers was remarkable. For example, real employee compensation per private employee in nonfarm establishments[78] rose steadily every year, and in 1945 was over one-fifth above the 1941 level. This reinforces the impression of firm gains for labor gleaned from the increases in real wage rates shown above. More broadly, similar results show up for the index of real disposable personal income per capita, which increased well over one-fourth during the same war years.[79] Although householders, as we know, were busy accumulating liquid and other assets out of this disposable income rise, they were also enjoying, on the average, an increase in consumption, as has been noted previously. Of course, it must always be borne in mind that any advances on the income side were associated with greater input effort on the cost side. Incidentally, it is noteworthy that reported work-injury frequency rates, with the exception of Class I railroads, were contained remarkably well in the commodity-producing activities.[80]

It has already been observed that farmers as a group fared well during the war. Farm size (in acres per farm) continued to trend upward, as did farm real estate values. Full and part ownership rose and tenancy declined. Equity per mortgaged farm jumped upward. Average per farm net income from farming doubled between 1941 and 1945.[81] Many marginal farm operators left agriculture and found comparatively lucrative jobs in the shipyards and other war industries. For farm laborers, monthly money wage rates, including board and room, rose from $34.50 to $79.00 over the same four years. Of course, while this represented a distinct gain relative to nonfarm workers, the level of annual wages was still far below that of nonfarm laborers. And the average per capita income of farm people from *all* sources in 1946 was still only 60 percent of that for nonfarm people.[82]

There were, of course, many other aspects, not touched upon above, that entered into the people's level of living and their quality of life, such as public safety, race discrimination and shocking antiblack violence, sex discrimination, and the reduced availability of "high culture." It would appear, however, that in none of these matters except racial violence was the behavioral pattern significantly different from immediate prewar patterns. Indeed, in the case of labor, violence against its organizational activities subsided noticeably as compared with the bitter depression years. A latter-day social issue of considerable magnitude — environmental pollution and deterioration — received then so little attention that practically nothing can be said of the wartime experience.

Income Distribution

The distribution of income does bear upon the underlying population's level of living, and the war did apparently produce a shift in that respect sufficient to warrant examination. And remarkably enough, those economists who specialize in that area seem to agree upon the "fact," with due apologies for estimating difficulties, of a moderate shift in the direction of greater equality, at least in the personal income distribution pattern.

The usual data refer to family personal annual money income (before taxes) received by families and unattached individuals, grouped into quintiles. The change may readily be seen by a comparison for selected years of the percentage distributions of national family income received by the lowest two quintiles taken together, and the highest quintile:[83]

	lowest 40%	highest fifth
1941	13.6%	48.8%
1944	15.8	45.8
1946	16.1	46.1
1947	16.0	46.0

| 1955 | 16.1 | 45.2 |
| 1962 | 15.5 | 45.5 |

Clearly, the notable change came between 1941 and 1944, and the distribution stabilized thereafter. The lowest two quintiles increased their proportionate share by 16 percent; the highest quintile's always large share fell by 6 percent. This change prompted a leading specialist to comment that "one of the heritages of the Great Depression and especially of World War II is an altogether new distribution of income by size."[84] Of course, the wartime shift in the pretax distribution of income by size does not negate the undoubted fact that "there were many individuals and families whose tax payments rose substantially more than income, and whose standards of living declined markedly."[85]

Another authority presented similar income estimates from various surveys for families only. Those data show the following percentage increases in average pretax money income per family from 1941 to 1945, again by quintiles:[86]

	increase
lowest 20%	111.5%
second 20	116.0
third 20	90.7
fourth 20	82.3
fifth 20	55.7
all families	76.7

The question, why the jump for the lower brackets and the relative drop for the highest, has challenged writers in the income distribution field. The importance of the question is heightened by the fact that the shift seems to have been a once-for-all matter, the move toward moderately greater equality having been pretty much arrested by the end of the war, as indicated by the figures above running into the early sixties, figures that could easily be extended with similar results through the seventies.

In an early *Economic Report of the President* after the war some explanations were forthcoming. These included, specifically with reference to 1946, the fact that there was high employment, a very high proportion of all jobs were on a full-time basis, and "many families . . . had more than one person gainfully employed."[87] These presumptions, of course, would have to apply most strongly to the lower income quintiles. It was also pointed out that during the war the share of income going to farmers, whose cash income was traditionally low relative to urban groups, had risen. Furthermore, wage rate increases from 1941 to 1946 were greatest in the lower wage brackets.[88] Finally, it may be noted that between 1941 and 1946, somewhat equalizing public transfer payments rose much more rapidly than personal income as a whole, while property incomes paid out (interest, profits, and rental income of persons) rose but slowly.

The question why some of the explanations for the wartime reduction in personal income inequality apply poorly in the postwar decades, i.e., how can one explain the stability after 1946, is more difficult. It would appear that the postwar decades did witness some mild movements in the distributive structure. One authority found, for example, that from the immediate postwar years to the 1960s there was some gain by the middle and upper part of the distribution relative to the lower groups and the upper tail.[89] But no leading writer has failed to note the clear shift toward equality wrought by the conditions of World War II.

Chapter Eight

The War's Consequences

THE STUDY OF the economy in World War II acquires a rich meaning for us only when its consequences are included in the inquiry. Although many of these consequences have already been treated, they and some others will be assembled in this chapter into a package in order to afford a more total view of the war's great impact on the economy. The totality of the war's economic effects is one of the chief reasons for choosing to explore the wartime experience. A number of the important concomitant effects of the war, such as the achievement of full employment, have been pointed out in the course of this book. There were other accompaniments whose meaning in the larger flow of economic history, such as the explosion of the veteran population, can fruitfully be extracted from the welter of events and subjected to a careful exploration. Some effects of the war emerged only in connection with related actions taken after V-J Day, in certain cases a considerable time after. These actions and their connections with the war experience also demand treatment as a single package with the war, regardless of the time lapse between the war's ending and such lagged actions.

We may conveniently distinguish two sometimes overlapping kinds of war consequence: (1) changes occuring in the economy and economic behavior, and (2) changes in policy. Consideration of these two types will be given in order.

There were specific wartime developments that had long-run unique effects. An example of this set is the emergence of important, war-induced new products, industries, and activities. The war economy greatly stimulated technological innovation. Perhaps the most prominent illustration is atomic power. The nuclear power industry was the offspring of the atom bomb. Radar and its industrial applications is another outstanding example of a wartime product with a significant industrial future. Many others could be listed, some of them products, some processes. Synthetic rubber production in large volume was both product and process innovation. It must be granted, however, that in the manufacturing sector the "production miracle" was accomplished largely on the basis of the preexisting system of industrial technology.

While technological advance was in some cases inhibited by wartime constraints, as with the new air conditioning industry, in other cases it was stimulated, as with color television and numerous innovations in motorized material-handling equipment.[1] Collier's *Year Book* for 1945 lists almost eight columns of war-connected innovations, or the activation and new application of older innovations, within the chemical industry alone, to say nothing of pharmaceuticals.[2] Outstanding examples were penicillin, synthetic quinine, atabrine, sulfa drugs, and the mass dissemination of DDT. Two studies by the Bureau of Labor Statistics of wartime technological developments for the Senate Military Affairs Committee listed over 2,300 items of wartime (although of course not necessarily war-induced) technical advance, many with postwar applications. Particular mention was given television, railroad radio telephony, other communications media, jet-propulsion and gas-turbine engines, plastics, synthetic rubber, and metal fabricating machinery and methods.[3]

Research activity by industry, as by government and the universities, was greatly enhanced under the high pressure of war needs. Large-scale research in electronics laid the basis for a postwar technological revolution. In the case of industry research, the prewar trend line was shifted dramatically upward. The National Research Council reported the existence of 2,450 industry research laboratories in 1947, employing 133,000 people, nearly twice the number of employees so engaged in 1940.[4] It was the war that instilled a new and heightened appreciation of scientific research. The link between science and technology was henceforth to become the hallmark of industrial progress in the postwar era.

There were additional changes wrought uniquely by the war that had lasting consequences. A second change unique to the war experience was the vast increase in the veteran population, a matter treated in the preceding chapter. In 1940 there were 4.3 million veterans in civil life; in 1950 there were 19 million. The effects of that tremendous increase were far reaching. For one thing, public outlays for veterans' education were almost nonexistent before World War II; but by 1947 over two and a quarter billion dollars were already being expended for that purpose. In this matter we are dealing with both a change in economic behavior and a war-induced policy development. The contribution of veterans' education to the training level of the U.S. labor force and to future technological advance was inestimable. We should also add here a reference to the improved quality of civil life enjoyed directly by those involved in the intellectually elevating process. The salutary spillover effects on the general population should also be acknowledged. Another repercussion, long delayed, however, was the explosive jump in veterans' health-care costs as the World War II contingent aged. It was that contingent (along with inflation), for example, that accounted for the rise in VA annual expenditures for medical, hospital, and domiciliary services from about $2 billion in 1970 to over $7 billion in 1981.[5] Congressional budget analysts projected that VA's annual medical bill could well exceed $15 billion by 1990.[6]

A third change in the economy specifically produced by war conditions, reiterated here in the interest of comprehensiveness, was the previously discussed "pre-fisc" (i.e., before any impact of government taxing and spending) shift in the distribution of income toward slightly greater equality. It needs to be emphasized that the shift was apparently a once-for-all economic change that was irrevocable. A fourth change, uniquely created by war restraints on wage increases, was the development of the fringe benefit in labor-management contracts. The fringe benefit was by no means entirely new, but its widespread adoption during the war gives it a special, war-related character. It too turned out to be an irreversible and enduring change, one that among other things greatly influenced development in the postwar labor movement.

Mention should also be made in this summation of two specific wartime developments in the policy field that revealed achievement possibilities heretofore not appreciated or well understood. These were the success of the government's incomes policy (i.e., price control) and the effectiveness of volunteer community effort under conditions viewed by the public as critical. If kept alive in the collective consciousness they are lessons that may prove useful at any appropriate social conjuncture.

Examination of the World War II economy has also revealed some abiding characteristics that were unaltered by the war except for the temporary, war-stimulated movement that they evinced. The first of such trends is population growth. The war eventuated in the baby boom, and the baby boom raised the total population rate substantially for a time. But only for a time: the long-run declining rate of American population growth was unaffected by that aberrant behavior pattern. A second similar war-connected deviation from trend was the jump in the economically significant women's labor force participation rate. Again, this proved to be episodic: it was an important but not a lasting consequence of the war. The third such event was government administrative direction of the economy. It did not turn out to be an abiding phenomenon, for that huge administrative apparatus was promptly dismantled. Economic planning was not to be the American way — at least for a long time to come. All that did turn out to be enduring, as will be discussed below, was a residue of government guidance generically resembling in a watered-down way what the French call "indicative planning." All that remained was the "mixed economy."

There were some economic trends or established characteristics of the system that were accelerated as they passed through the wartime environment; and these particular changes were not, like the hump in the female participation rate trend, temporary. They were long lasting. It is tempting to mention the political example of the expansion in the executive power in the federal government, a speeding up of a trend instituted by the New Deal. But there are at least two more economic illustrations. One is clearly economic: the acceleration in black out-migration from agriculture and from the South, together with the very large black occupational shifts, men into industry, women out of domestic service and into both industry and commercial services. The wartime FEPC inaugurated a growing movement toward civil rights and fair employment practices.

A second example is provided by the wartime upsurge of business influence in government. During the war the Pentagon and the State Department were strongly infiltrated by Wall Street elements, a business stratum that to a substantial degree directed foreign policy into an anti-Soviet groove after the war. The central role of business during the war also terminated both the public disillusionment with business attendent upon the Great Depression experience, and the labor orientation of government under the New Deal. As has been shown, the enduring effectiveness of business influence is expressed in such postwar phenomena as the Taft-Hartley and Landrum-Griffin laws and the formation of what President Eisenhower termed the "military-industrial complex." By the same token, reference to the two main pieces of postwar "labor" legislation is a reminder that the considerable participation of organized labor representatives in the wartime administrative machinery marked the completion of the process whereby business generally came to accept, subject to retraction should a shift in power relations occur, unionization and collective bargaining as permanent institutions in the market system. A third aspect of this legislation will be discussed below.

War, the Mixed Economy, and America's New Global Role

The war brought both accelerated change and the reshaping of domestic and foreign economic policy on the part of the federal government. These alterations in policy were at least as portentous as the whole collection of changes in the economy itself. On the domestic front, the war was a connecting rod between the New Deal's inauguration of the mixed economy and its quite unexpected crystallization during a span of a very few years following V-J Day. It is worth remembering that most Americans had probably believed the assumption of some measure of government responsibility for the economy's performance was only a cyclical, pump-priming episode.

On the foreign policy front, the war was responsible for (1) abrogating the temporary cooperation between the U.S. and the USSR that had reached a degree of closeness never achieved before or since; and (2) a vigorous presumption by the United States government that it must assume vast new responsibilities for world order, responsibilities that before the war were not dreamed of even in nonisolationist circles.

Domestic Policy

Unnoticed by almost everybody, a quietly growly domestic trend in the economy and in policy, a trend of lasting character, had been taking place since 1929. The proportion of personal consumption expenditures to GNP in current dollars had been 74.8 percent in 1929; in 1949 that proportion had fallen to 71.0 percent; and in 1946 it was down to 68.6 percent.[7] The surprising concomitant was an offsetting rise in the ratio of all government purchases to GNP, together with a gross fixed business nonresidential investment ratio (domestic) that remained in the long run persistently about constant at the 1929 level of some 10 percent. In the emerging U.S. mixed economy private consumption was steadily yielding to collective (i.e, social, via government) consumption and *leaving the long-run private investment ratio unaffected* as compared with its laissez-faire antecedent. The irreversible march of big government, while no doubt but dimly anticipated by most, was clearly under way during the reconversion period.[8]

The proportion of the labor force employed in the civilian public sector was rising along with the government budget. Meanwhile, it was expected that the Employment Act of 1946, proposed in embryo form as early as 1943 by the National Resources Planning Board, would guard against future recessionary episodes. And fortunately for the prescience shown on the public revenue side, the wartime addition of many millions of lower-income people to the federal taxpayer contingent[9] had laid the foundation for big expenditures in the future. This same new tax (and expenditures) structure also created a "built-in," countercyclical stabilizer and slightly reshaped the distribution of income. The built-in stabilizers successfully passed their first test in the mild recession and revival of 1948–49. The 1946 government guarantee of maximum employment and purchasing power was an almost revolutionary commitment unprecedented in the history of government's relation to the economy. On the surface at least, the Congress was announcing that it would indefinitely underwrite high-level aggregate business sales, aggregate profits, the total wage bill, and economic growth in the context of a growing labor force.

The welfare state component of the budget in the now fixated era of big government was complemented in the U.S. case by the huge military outlays necessitated by what was to turn out to be a permanent Cold War, initiated shortly after the cessation of World War II. The big Cold War and associated hot war military budgets made very large total budgets chronic and sullied the historic notion of a peacetime economy. Military appropriations soon acquired an almost sacrosanct status before a willing Congress, so that the persistent attacks on absolutely growing federal budgets in the decades following World War II were largely explicit or implicit assaults upon the civilian component — which meant, for the most part, the welfare component.

Such assaults were directly rooted in the earliest controversial years of the infant mixed economy, when the New Deal's fledgling income security programs were held at bay by its laissez-faire adversaries. Had the U.S. mixed economy found it necessary to maintain high aggregate demand for employment through overwhelmingly civilian federal purchases of goods and services, as was notably more the case with the European mixed economies, the institutionalization of the new social consensus would probably have enjoyed the security of firmer foundations. The welfare state would have had to advance more rapidly, e.g., in the area of health insurance. Furthermore, Keynesian aggregate demand management (such as it was) would have been freer of the erratic influences on the federal budget emanating from the response of the military budget to the vicissitudes of cold and hot wars. After all, the size and the domestic economic impact of the military budget was not *supposed* to be an integral part of demand management.

Nevertheless, it was a most remarkable aspect of the history of the mixed-economy federal budgets that civilian plus military expenditures, when added to large and growing state and local expenditures, were sufficient to maintain a generally high level of employment and to avoid severe depressions.

The implied "inner logic" of this remarkable historical relationship involved in summing the military and civilian components of the all-government budgets has never been revealed, although it may be hypothesized that much controversy over welfare outlays was minimized or avoided by a heavy reliance upon defense outlays. But the broad pattern can be observed. In the first half-decade after World War II that pattern had barely emerged. But it did emerge.

It was of great historic significance that the war did not call into question the basics of the major legislative achievements identified with the New Deal. This was true, for example, of the minimum wage law, the Social Security Act, and the National Labor Relations Act. However, in two areas postwar actions were taken that properly warrant some treatment regarding how the pertinent New Deal policies fared as a result of the wartime experience and the immediately consequent crystallization of the mixed system. The two areas referred to are farm policy and government's role in labor-management relations.

Farm Policy

It was, of course, widely hoped and believed in the early New Deal years that the farm price support program, like some of the other depression aids for farmers, was a temporary protective program for a disadvantaged group. The Agricultural Adjustment Act of 1933 was presented to the Congress and the public as an emergency measure, although the Roosevelt administration soon became increasingly conscious of the long-run character of the farm income problem.[10] This should have been evident from the historical record of agricultural-industrial disparity, the war's demonstration that the nation could get along with a lot less farms, the chronic farm agitation in the United States, and the widespread practice in other industrialized countries of public support for the agrarian interest.

During and immediately after the war the post–World War I chronic problems of farm commodity surpluses was reversed, and the overall ratio of prices received to prices paid by farmers jumped to a high of 115 in 1947. Nevertheless, it was asserted in 1948 that there would be a "continuing need for crop insurance and for storage programs for staples and marketing programs for perishables"; and furthermore, that commodity price supports were a desideratum for protection against "special dislocations which might arise in case of recession."[11] In line with these policy precepts the Agricultural Act of 1948, as amended in 1949, quickly fastened securely the now traditional price support program for "basic," "Steagall," and "other" commodities upon the farm policy of the United States.[12] At the same time, more flexible price-support levels (75 to 90 percent of parity, the percentage varying inversely with current levels of supply) in place of the rigid 90 percent supports previously obtaining were introduced, and the calculation of the parity-price formula was brought up to date. Actually, the flexible provisions did not become operative for some time.

Interwoven with and underlying the price-quantity program of supply management was the abiding farm-nonfarm divergence in per capita real income. The Council of Economic Advisers acknowledged the related necessity for a permanent public policy to deal with this in its January 1953 *Annual Economic Review*, declaring that "the sound objective of 'parity for agriculture' has not yet been achieved," and "many vigorous things will need to be done on a broad front to enable the farm population to have a standard of living and a degree of opportunity closer to that of other groups . . ."[13] Subsequent history abundantly showed that this expectation was endowed with much prescience, and a complex package of government domestic and foreign trade supports, especially for the "basic" 50 percent of all crop and livestock products, became a prominent hallmark of the evolving postwar interventionist regime.

Labor, Government, and Unionism

The Wagner Labor Relations Act of 1935 had established the policy that economically important industrial disputes were, like "natural monopolies" in the utility field, "affected with a public interest." The mixed economy in the fields of industrial relations and unionism therefore extended the long arm of government to reach deeper and deeper into union-management affairs. The two major pieces of federal amending legislation referred to above were the chief vehicles of a stepped-up extension of this trend after World War II. Management forces found sufficient willing allies in the Republican-controlled Congress to push through (over the President's veto) the Taft-Hartley amendment to the Wagner Act by exploiting the fear produced by the enormous wartime growth of union membership, the increase in market and political power of organized labor, the strike waves of 1944–46, and the accompanying spread of contracts with compulsory membership provisions. The American antipathy for concentration of power in business was readily transmitted by Senator Taft, of "maximum employment" fame, to bigness in labor organization. It was now less plausible to view organized labor as a disadvantaged group.

But the aspect emphasized at this point is not so much the pro-employer character of what labor called a "slave labor" law. Rather it is the spur that the Labor-Management Relations Act of 1947 gave to governmental intrusion into the labor-management arena, a fact that was pointed out in President Truman's veto message. The flavor of the new, high level of public involvement may be gleaned from a paraphrasing of certain provisions of a law that greatly augmented government's task from *assuring the process* of collective bargaining to *regulating the terms* of collective bargaining settlements.[14] Under those provisions, employee conduct was now restricted by the numerous stipulations laid down in six categories of "unfair" union practices in this amending act that more or less paralleled the original act's "unfair" employer practices. The act's requirement, as interpreted, that the services of the NLRB would be available only to unions whose officers signed noncommunist affidavits, represented an intrusion of the Cold War into labor's affairs, an intrusion more than vigorously matched by labor's own leadership through a campaign that shortly destroyed effective communist influence in the labor movement.

The federal government was now required to supervise and enforce alleged union malpractices, and was now committed to protect *individual employees* against unfair union practices that were presumed to infringe upon their rights. Restrictions also were laid down with respect to the methods of handling political finances and union welfare funds; union behavior in jurisdictional disputes between two or more unions; and "excessive" or "discriminatory" initiation fees. Constraints were stipulated regarding union participation in secondary boycotts (pressuring an employer not involved in the dispute who can influence the employer who is). Provision was also made for presidential intervention in "national emergency" disputes.[15] Under the aegis of these regulations the federal government became a silent or overt participant in many disputes connected with interstate commerce and also in the management of union affairs.

It was the Taft-Hartley provision outlawing union contracts providing for a closed shop (i.e., only union members can be hired) that was picked up in particular in the ensuing spate of additional state "right-to-work" laws. In fact, Taft-Hartley was the enabling act permitting passage of such laws, and the states adopting such legislation usually extended the prohibition to almost all forms of compulsory union membership, including the union shop, maintenance-of-membership clauses, and preferential hiring. About twenty states passed such laws after 1947, largely in the South and West, where union organization was weak. These states thus advanced another step toward the thriving regime of public intervention. However, only Indiana among the big industrial states passed a right-to-work law, and probably without being aware of the somewhat ironic probability that once statutory protection was extended, and reaffirmed by Taft-Hartley, to the right of workers to organize unions of their own choice and to bargain with employers collectively, they had little need for compulsory membership contracts to preserve their unions.[16]

The Landrum-Griffin Act, or Labor-Management Reporting Act, was passed in 1959, prompted by the widely publicized union corrupt practices in a few unions as revealed by Senator John McClellan's "Select Committee on Improper Activities in the Labor or Management Field."[17] While this additional amendment to the National Labor Relations Act of 1935 does not fall chronologically into the immediate postwar period, it was a functional extension of the public policy represented by the growing body of major labor laws in the now firmly established mixed economy. The thrust of Landrum-Griffin was to broaden considerably Taft-Hartley's inroads into the internal operations of labor unions in the name of protecting the individual member against the union officialdom.

Landrum-Griffin requires

the filing of reports describing the organization, financial dealings, and business practices of labor organizations, their officers and employees, certain employers, labor relations consultants, and unions in trusteeship; safeguards union election procedures; sets standards for the handling of union funds, . . . closes previously existing loopholes in the protection against secondary boycotts; and limits organizational and jurisdictional picketing.[18]

These union reports were to be made available to public examination. Under Title 5 individual members could bring suit against union officials for alleged improprieties in financial management or other aspects of a union official's activities. Trusteeships, under which a national union might assume control over a local, were also subject to federal oversight. The act created thirteen new federal crimes, eight new civil remedies, and ten new enforcement procedures.[19]

It was therefore to be expected that the National Labor Relations Board administering these laws would become one of the major regulatory agencies of the federal government. In 1980 the NLRB estimated annual expenditures exceeded the anticipated budgets of the Civil Aeronautics Board, Interstate Commerce Commission, Federal Trade Commission, and Securities and Exchange Commission, and was over twice as large as the budget of the Antitrust Division of the Justice Department.[20] The agency had 50 field offices by the end of 1979, its annual case intake load (unfair labor practice charges plus representation elections) having jumped from about 15,000 a year in the fifties to 31,000 in 1969 and about 55,000 ten years later.[21] Its total financial outlays rose from almost $13 million in the year of Landrum-Griffin's passage to over $100 million in fiscal 1979.[22] Even if these expenditure totals are converted into 1972 dollars,[23] the real outlay rise over that twenty-year period was 169 percent. As one authority expressed it prophetically at the end of the sixties,

If free bargaining is rendered futile by the hopes of each side that government intervention eventually will work to its benefit and if government is increasingly unwilling to tolerate the end result of unsuccessful mediation, then government in the future will be forced increasingly to dictate settlement terms.[24]

While it was not necessarily as clear who would "dictate" terms, certain it was that labor-management relations, like so many other so-called private economic activities, became thoroughly "mixed" with government already upon the passage of Taft-Hartley in that eventful 1947.

The Great Reversal to Internationalism

Domestic interventionism in the now fixated mixed economy after the war was complemented by a transformation to an era of globalism in foreign policy. Considerable attention is devoted to that transformation in this last chapter for two reasons: first because of its enormous historical importance, and second because there is no treatment of the matter earlier in this book. The changeover to internationalism was induced by the onset of the long-lived Cold War and the closely related U.S. concern with the direction to be taken by the flows of world trade and investment together with politicoeconomic evolution in the restive Third World countries. Big Cold War and then hot war military budgets in the United States made large total federal budgets a certainty, and tarnished the traditional concept of a "peacetime economy."

The Cold War was a byproduct of World War II that enhanced an anti-Soviet tradition dating far back to the Russian Revolution. The post–World War II upsurge grew out of the weakening of the prewar European military power that had functioned as a capitalist buffer against the socialist Soviet giant. The specter of a communist Europe coming out of a world war had terrified France and Britain before the war, and had led them to favor peace at the price of almost any concession to the Nazis, such as the loss of Czechoslovakia that was negotiated at Munich in 1938. As the German ambassador to Paris reported in May of that fateful year, French Foreign Minister Georges Bonnet "considered any arrangement better than world war, in the event of which all Europe would perish, and both victor and vanquished would fall victims to world communism."[25]

It had been widely believed before the war that the USSR was a paper tiger, but the demonstrated Soviet capability in the war changed all that. The similar war-enhanced U.S. economic and military capability, in the setting of a prostrated, devasted Europe open to a real or fancied threat in several places by a combination of indigenous and Soviet-supported communism, made the United States the apparent choice among the great capitalist powers to contain the socialist threat to the institution of private property and the capitalist order everywhere. This newly assumed responsibility determined the essential, although not the entire, character of postwar internationalism. As one historian of postwar foreign policy expressed it:

The internationalists . . . by substituting anticommunism for the moral imperative of internationalism in the first postwar years . . . clinched their argument at a time when foreign intervention could be quite clearly defined as helping European states under threat . . .

Two conditions, then, prevented a thoughtful sifting of American interests and opportunities after World War II: the need to mobilize American political consent for an international role and the obtrusiveness of the Soviet Communist enemy. Furthermore, it became prudent for every presidential administration to adopt a cover-all-bets strategy toward the Communist world, which included support of anti-Communists all over the globe . . .[26]

The U.S. policy, rejecting at that juncture a spheres-of-influence approach and favoring self-determination for the Eastern European countries bordering the USSR (American "universalism"), was seen by the Soviets as an effort to reopen those adjacent states to hostile capitalistic penetration. From then on the continued overt and covert wars involving the peculiar universalisms of the two superpowers all across the globe were fought taking those two perspectives as starting point, i.e., to give self-determination, particularly for countries in the now largely decolonized Third World, a character and direction desired by the respective contestants.

The major U.S. moves came in quick succession: enunciation of the Truman Doctrine in 1947, followed by its three chief instrumentalities, the Marshall Plan (1947) to reconstitute and stabilize Europe economically and politically, NATO (inaugurated 1949), and Point Four (1949) to stabilize and stimulate development in the Third World economies. Some years later but in the same vein, President Kennedy inaugurated in response to Fidel Castro's Cuba the Alliance for Progress for Latin America. There were also two hot, overt wars — Korea and

Vietnam. U.S. armed forces after the major World War II demobilization never again fell below about 1.5 million, and the military
budget had already begun its long-run rise in 1948.

The Organization of International Order

The last years of the war brought the establishment through the
newly created United Nations of a number of institutions for stabilizing
the foreign exchanges, structuring multilateral trade between the advanced countries, and providing loans for reconstruction or economic
development. An international conference of the Western bloc at Bretton Woods, New Hampshire, in July 1944 laid the groundwork for
the three leading postwar institutions, the most important of which
was the International Monetary Fund (IMF), established at the end
of 1945 and already operating two years later. The major and, as it
turned out, paradoxical purpose of the IMF was to try to ensure short-
period foreign exchange rate stability without the sacrifice by member
countries of domestic high employment goals.

In addition to the IMF, the Bretton Woods conference led to the
establishment of a permanent International Bank for Reconstruction
and Development (IBRD, December 1945) designed chiefly to facilitate "sound," commercial project loans to member governments; and
an international trade organization that after considerable tortuous
negotiating became converted into the makeshift but lasting General
Agreement on Tariffs and Trade (GATT, at Geneva in March 1947).
GATT survived the stillbirth of a more formal international trade
organization to become the chief vehicle for informal collective efforts
to reduce trade restrictions.

All the arrangements may be viewed as extensions into the international arena of the management of economic performance by governments, and as mincing steps toward a future global regime of in-
tergovernmental planning that would attempt to reconcile the conflicts
between the goals of the domestic mixed systems and the foreign
economic policies of the leading Western countries and regional economic communities. In what turned out to be the historically early

stages in the evolution of these endeavors, the Third World initially received most subordinate consideration. Thus, the Bretton Woods institutions crystallized not only the great schism between the West and the Soviet bloc but also a certain patronizing, de facto indifference to the long-term developmental needs of the less developed countries (LDCs).[27] Soon, however, the Cold War and the clamor of the LDCs forced the industrialized nations to relinquish some of that indifference.

The IMF, like the other Bretton Woods–type organizations that subsequently developed,[28] was set up to try to overcome some of the defects plaguing the interwar, international economy—the breakdown of the gold standard, competitive devaluations and depreciations, trade restrictions, beggar-my-neighbor polices, etc. The Fund's monetary resources, upon which members could draw, consisted of a gold sum, U.S. dollars, and members' currencies, as provided by each country in accordance with its fixed quota based upon weights determined by its world trade share, national income, and population. The official exchange rate parities of all countries were defined in terms of *both* gold and dollars, thus acknowledging the world dominance of the dollar over the pound in foreign exchange. In effect, the new system set up an international gold exchange standard (convertibility of a country's currency into the currency of a gold-standard nation) with a high ratio of foreign exchange to gold. The "gold-dollar standard" might be a more appropriate term, reflecting the "key currency" role of the dollar.

The Fund's chief declared goals were to promote exchange rate "stability without rigidity," especially by helping members finance short-run payments deficits; to monitor members' exchange rate policies so as to avoid both predatory exchange depreciation and domestic deflation/unemployment; and (hopefully) to provide for adjustment of foreign exchange rates (but not for unlimited amounts of foreign exchange) in the event of long-run "fundamental disequilibria." This was clearly a big order, reflecting "the heavy negotiation that went into it and the multifarious and not easily reconciled objectives its creators had in mind."[29]

The objectives implied a visionary world largely free of both domestic controls imposed under balance-of-payments pressures and, related thereto, debtor positions mounting in magnitude year after year if deficits persisted. The debtor-creditor conflict lay behind the clash between Britain's Keynes Plan for an international money ("bancor") which debtors could obtain without specified limits, and the successfully propounded U.S. White Plan for the above-mentioned currency pool.[30] The United States feared that under the Keynes Plan, and in the context of the existing world dollar shortage, overdrafts of bancor would in effect require it to extend dollar credits that eventually would turn out to be gifts.[31] Britain, on the other hand, correctly feared that the pound, and its balance of payments in general, was in mortal danger from its lost empire income and its vanished export competitiveness. It is ironic that when the Bretton Woods "fixed but adjustable" exchange rate finally collapsed, after a long illness, in 1971–73, the new world money unit, called "Special Drawing Rights," came to bear a close family resemblance to Britain's bancor.

Because of the legacy of international disruption left by the war, the IMF provided for an unstipulated period of transition "during which its members were not to be restrained by the Fund's prohibition against exchange controls. That interlude continued "far beyond the period of post-war disequilibrium,"[32] during which "extensive exchange controls were the order of the day."[33] Meanwhile, the Fund insisted, most prematurely, in September 1946 that every member declare a par value for its currency. The result was a rash of overvalued currencies that had to be adjusted downward in a wave of devaluations exactly three years later. The pound fell from $4.03 to $2.80, over 30 percent. In no other way could Europe's devastated economies, in the face of the dollar shortage and their gold losses, hope to generate the necessary exports;[34] and the IMF, significantly, had to passively welcome those desperate but reasonable moves. The Marshall Plan had been quite inadequate to correct the enormous trade disparities. Indeed, the United Kingdom had already as early as August 1947 faced a "convertibility crisis," involving the stoppage of sterling convertibility, after a gold-and-dollar reserve drop of almost $1 billion over the preceding seven months.[35] The Fund's goal of a global multilateral system had to be postponed for years, and it made few large-scale loans between 1947 and 1956. In the latter year of continuing dollar shortages the Suez Canal was closed owing to hostilities between Egypt and Israel-Britain-France, and the Fund made available about $1 billion of "standby credits." The period of comparative inactivity thus ended. But as the end of the fifties approached, new challenges to the Fund's stability goals were developing as a result of world inflation, the American comparative productivity lag, the upcoming Euro-Japanese invasion of world markets, and the impending transformation from dollar shortage to dollar glut.

With respect to the IBRD's grand conservative design to assist in the reconstruction, restoration, and development of advanced war-torn as well as less developed IMF member countries, actual accomplishment was for many years less than impressive — loans approximating $4.5 billion to all areas over the twelve years from its inception to June 30, 1959.[36] Insufficiency was particularly acute during those years of quiescence in the case of long-term loans to LDCs, which were constrained by the high risk involved, the requirement that only "project" loans be extended, and the rule that only the foreign exchange portion of a total project's costs could be financed by the Bank. The Bank found it necessary to create offspring, such as the International Development Association (IDA), to correct its failures vis-à-vis the LDCs. Subsequently, the Bank together with the IDA and the International Finance Corporation (IFC) came to be known as the "World Bank Group," with the IDA concentrating on the very poorest countries. The IFC evolved into a "relatively insignificant appendage" to the Bank and the IDA.[37] The IDA was not restricted to project loans and was better adapted to provide "soft" loans (low to zero interest, longer maturities, repayment in local currencies, and waivers of payment in the case of balance-of-payments difficulties) that would yield political rather than hard economic returns.[38] The IBRD idea, rooted like all the Bretton Woods structures in the conditions recalled from the Great Depression years, was locked into the objective of merely channeling long-term capital in a steadier and more regular flow than private capital markets had previously provided.[39]

This was not adequate to meet even a moderate part of the developmental requirements of the Third World. As late as 1965 the president of the World Bank Group, referring to international capital provision to the LDCs from *all* sources including his own agency, declared that the present level of finance is wholly inadequate, whether measured by the growth rate which the advanced countries say they are willing to facilitate [i.e., 1 percent of national income] or in terms of the amount of external capital which the developing countries have demonstrated they can use effectively.[40]

It must be acknowledged that the role of the IBRD and the later World Bank Group had to compete with a wave of bilateral and multilateral grants and soft loans with strong political attachments. Not that the IBRD was during its first quarter century or so by any means independent of U.S. national interests: its presidents were U.S. citizens, its headquarters were in Washington, the top members of its highly centralized staff were Americans, its chief decisions were made in Washington rather than in the field, "all stages of the project cycle were managed from Washington," country economic reports were prepared in Washington,[41] and, by way of example, specified disbursements by borrowers for imports from the United States on a cumulative basis through June 30, 1960 constituted one-half of all loan expenditures.[42] Alan S. Milward concluded that as early as 1947 the IBRD and the IMF had become "subordinated to United States control and operated no longer in the universal interest but as instruments of United States policy."[43] President Eisenhower's plans to make the IBRD and private lenders the mainstay of U.S. and perhaps world development assistance was sidetracked by the Cold War. Nevertheless, the World Bank Group was gradually giving more development direction and increasing the number of loans and credits to LDCs, in somewhat larger amounts, by the late sixties; disbursements of the Bank and IDA over the decade 1967–76 averaged over $1.7 billion annually.[44]

GATT was dedicated to reducing constraints on trade, the IMF to constraints on payments, an economically artificial separation.[45] The chief U.S. long-run objective in supporting an international organization devoted to the reduction of tariffs was to increase exports. As Benjamin Disraeli once said, "free trade is not a principle, it is an expedient." By virtue of its great productivity advantage at the end of the war, the United States was willing, as it was under the reciprocal trade agreements program of the New Deal, to negotiate concessions regarding imports in order to get freer access to foreign markets, especially after the "transition" period devoted to rebuilding Europe's export trade. By linking tariff negotiations with most-favored-nation (MFN) treatment that automatically extended the concessions to most other trading partners, successive extensions of the 1934 Trade Agreements Act empowered the President to maintain through GATT negotiations the U.S. position of free multilateral trade advocate. Such a role was not fundamentally compromised by the American preference for minimizing the impact of MFN by limiting its concessions in most important cases to products of which the other negotiator was the principal supplier. Also, tariff concessions by the United States did open up more of the U.S. market, and reciprocal concessions embracing MFN by foreign countries opened up foreign markets to the United States.

By the transfer of negotiations from the bilateral form with MFN, as under the original Trade Agreements Act, to GATT's international arena involving about 90 percent of world trade, the cause of expanding multilateral exchange was somewhat better served. With almost forty countries participating in the ensuing tariff-reduction "rounds" the loose-knit congressionally unratified, nonpermanent, almost memberless association gradually became elevated, in the words of Secretary of State Dean Rusk, to "a code of conduct for fair play in international trade."[46]

Originally the participants from the industrially advanced countries grudgingly acknowledged that there was some justification for exempting the LDCs from GATT's antiprotectionist program. But by the late fifties, under pressure from the LDCs, they were openly released from other than nominal adherence to free trade principles, on the assumption, of course, that they would exercise reasonable restraint.[47]

Certain actual or potential threats over the long run to the free trade goal of GATT, aside from the usual "exceptions" provisions, were formally incorporated into the agreement. Probably the main actual threat was the provision, inserted at the behest of the United States particularly, that quotas could be applied to restrict imports of farm products that were subject to domestic price support programs. This exclusion of agricultural policies from GATT rules plagued that body (but not those participants who had farm programs) throughout the postwar decades. Indeed, in the area of import quotas generally, GATT goals were vulnerable because while such restraints were disallowable for *protective* purposes they were allowable during the "postwar transition period" for balance-of-payments purposes!

The "transitional period" policy also developed into a threat after the late fifties because a number of important countries continued to maintain quantitative import restrictions that were originally imposed ostensibly for balance-of-payments reasons even though such alleged reasons were no longer applicable.[48]

An additional danger to GATT objectives, one that turned out not to be particularly operative, was the inclusion of the U.S. Trade Agreements Act's "peril point" and "escape clause" stipulations providing for withdrawal or reduction of already negotiated tariff concessions whenever some import might injure a domestic industry.

A final major potential threat, one that many at the turn of the sixties believed had emerged with the formation of the European Economic Community (EEC, Common Market) in 1957–58, was the innocent-sounding Article XXIV permitting departure from MFN treatment in the case of customs unions and free trade groupings, i.e., integrated trading blocs. The United States favored this provision of GATT in 1947 in the belief that such unions would probably be stepping stones to increased multilateral trade among countries having payments difficulties. But the EEC "threatened the U.S. balance-of-payments position in two ways—directly, through tariff discrimination against U.S. exports, and indirectly, through the attractions of a booming protected European market to U.S. direct and portfolio investment."[49] The subsequent invasion of Europe by U.S. multinational corporations bore out this latter expectation, but the extent to which a threat developed was not easily or immediately appraised.[50] On the matter of tariff discrimination, it was estimated, for example, that the Common Market's agricultural policy became significantly more protectionist than the previous individual country restrictions on agricultural imports — a clear violation of GATT principles.[51] A more subtle, nontariff barrier to trade emanating from the Common Market was de facto tax discrimination.[52] The EEC also adopted special tariff preferences in exchange for "reverse preferences" with 19 of its former African colonies and with various other nations.[53]

Table 8.1
Trends in the Relative Importance of Tariff Collections, *by Value*, Selected Years

	Duties collected / Total imports	Duties collected / Dutiable imports	Dutiable imports / Total imports
1931	18%	53%	33%
1941	14	37	37
1949	6	14	41
1959	7	12	61
1970	7	10	65
1978	4	6	70
1982	4	5	69

SOURCE: Data from *Historical Statistics*, pt. 2, p. 888, ser. 207, 209, 211, 212; *Statistical Abstract*, 1979, p. 871, no. 1519, and 1984, p. 841, no. 1477.

GATT was clearly a bold venture that confronted enormous odds. Its subsequent history revealed both modest achievements and failures. Its participants were constantly engaged in a struggle between declared goals and the determination of governments to protect their balance of payments regardless of those goals, especially when U.S. payments deficits were no longer needed to build up the gold and dollar exchange reserves of European countries. On the whole, the generally liberal trade policies followed by the United States in the quarter-century after World War II, largely through the instrumentality of GATT, helped expand U.S. exports and imports and thus contributed to rising per capita incomes and a wider choice of products both at home and abroad.[54]

The U.S. tariff and trade record from the end of the war to the end of the "transitional" dollar shortage period, marked by the formation of the EEC in 1959 and the advent of formal convertibility of the major European currencies into dollars in 1958, provides a limited empirical test of the early impact of trade liberalization policy, and possibly also of GATT.

The tariff revenue record seems consistent with the declared U.S. policy of reduced protection. Through the bilateral negotiations before War II and the multilateral bargaining after the war until 1953, i.e., over the first twenty years of the trade agreements program, the average ad valorem equivalent of U.S. duties was cut in half.[55] Table 8.1 shows the trends in the relative importance of tariff collections. The last few years are inserted for historical comparison. While the interpretation is not unambiguous, it seems clear that in the aggregate tariff revenues were a sharply declining influence upon the flow of products from abroad into the U.S. market. The last column of the table suggests that imports were levied upon more and more of the goods entering the United States as time passed; but comparison with the first two columns indicates that the rates applied were getting ever lower. The policy was not tariff elimination, but drastic tariff reduction.

It is also evident that the big tariff cuts were made by 1949, and that during the 1950s GATT could not have been accomplishing much in the way of liberalization. Of course, there was a lead time of up to a decade between negotiated tariff reductions and their effective implementation. But the trend series of weighted average rates in table 8.1 (first two columns) shows nothing very significant happening in the sixties either. There is only a gentle downward drift in the percentage of duties collected to dutiable imports over the two decades from 1949 to 1970. It is not until the seventies, after the implementation of GATT's Kennedy Round negotiations, "by far the most comprehensive in history."[56] that there was another significant drop in the percentages of duties collected shown in the first two columns.

Nevertheless, it seems likely that GATT created a more favorable set of circumstances for reciprocal tariff reductions than obtained under the old bilateral pattern of negotiation. One analyst concluded, for example, that it was doubtful if the old pattern "would have resulted in the added reduction in American tariff levels which occurred between 1948 and 1953."[57] Although the impact of GATT may have been marginal as compared with bilateralism, that it was positive seems plausible. Plausibility is enhanced by the likely circumstance that almost all the industrialized countries stood to gain from more international competition in the context of an American policy dedicated to strengthening the economies of the noncommunist world.

Still, the extent of GATT's impact cannot be isolated from all other influences affecting the actual trade pattern in the decade and a half from 1945 to the end of the fifties. This period is selected because it marks a time span that exhibited a somewhat cohesive and distinctive phase of international experience and policy. These were the early Cold War years of the new Bretton Woods organizations, the dollar shortage, U.S. policy to help rebuild the war-shattered industrial economies presumed to be politically threatened, undervalued and inconvertible European currencies, and frighteningly insufficient international reserves abroad, years prior to the formation of EEC, years of relatively superior U.S. productivity. Above all and specifically the United States wanted to lose some ground in international trade in favor of the other industrial economies, while at the same time contributing to its own domestic economic health.

The viable international organizations that came out of the 1944 Bretton Woods conference represented in the early postwar years, like the United Nations itself, a historically more advanced stage of cooperation than had been possible in the era of laissez-faire and the old gold standard. For all their weaknesses and their ties with the foreign economic policies of the major Western powers, these organizations inaugurated an era of encroachment upon national sovereignties that, at a new and higher level of economic management, paralleled the concomitant spread of the multinational corporation. This encroachment came to be perceived only gradually, grudgingly, and dimly as an essential complement to domestic demand management.

In other words, as piecemeal planning evolved toward more comprehensive planning on the national plane, so did planned international integration proceed along with it. This interpretation, which highlights the link between these two components of government interventionism in the postwar world, is insightfully advanced also by the eminent Swedish economist Assar Lindbeck, who notes several historically new and relevant features of the world economy: revolutionary developments in communications technology; the internationalization of entrepreneurship and technology in general; an increase in foreign trade shares within practically all private production sectors; the fact that the externalities like air and ocean pollution have become external to *nations*—not only, as earlier, to firms and households; and the deepening *awareness* of international interdependence.[58] He then draws the implied conclusion:

the tension between international economic forces and domestic policy ambitions is much more strongly felt today than in earlier periods because the domestic political objectives have become so much more numerous, detailed, and ambitious. Economic interdependence was not a serious economic policy problem before governments established targets concerning domestic variables

such as employment, growth, inflation, income distribution, and the allocation of resources . . . Experience during the post–World War II period
has also shown that strategic domestic stabilization policy *target* variables are
strongly influenced by fluctuations abroad in output and prices . . .

All this illustrates, of course, the need of conceiving both macro analysis
and stabilization policy in an international context.[59]

The fact that the private sector of the mixed economies in the postwar
world was considerably more internationalized than it was in the past,
when added to the rise of big government, created new and stronger
imperatives to tie in domestic (management) policies with foreign economic policy. Consequently, for example, regarding the foreign exchange rate, one authority distinguished the thirties and the early
Bretton Woods period, when policy stress was upon the role of exchange rates in improving external competitiveness, from later years
when the shift in real resources between the domestic and the foreign
sectors through exchange rate adjustments had to be coordinated with
government demand management and with domestic cost and price
policies.[60] Also, the trade-off over time between exchange rate policy
and monetary policy designed to achieve domestic price stability had
to be managed to the extent feasible. Furthermore, the economic
relations within the industrialized world, and between the latter and
the Third World, required increasingly deliberate and coordinated
measures in order to try to "rationalize" disequilibrium and rivalry.
The Bretton Woods organizations, despite their tradition-laden orientation at the outset, tried to inaugurate, each in its own way, specialized responses to those planning imperatives.

An Era Authenticated by War

There was much more to World War II than the war itself. For the
United States, the integral parts of that great upheaval were not only
the handful of vital changes occurring between 1941 and 1945; even
more vital for the long run were the momentous policy developments
during the few subsequent years of the war decade.

The leading contours of a whole postwar policy era were crystallized in that short span of years following the war's end. Those contours have been briefly outlined in this chapter: historically large public budgets with a huge military component at the federal level; the welfare state element; publicly underwritten employment, output, and growth; stabilization of the economic cycle; the intrusion of government as a third party in labor-management relationships; supply management in agriculture; and vigorous U.S. participation in a new, higher level of international organization together with the unfolding Cold War.

These policies on the domestic plane became identified with the demand management phase of the evolving mixed economy—the phase whose transformation into a later stage was inaugurated by the crisis of stagflation (inflation with stagnant performance) and its attendant policy crisis threatening the Keynesian system of public management. When the stagflation crisis did develop in the seventies, the established interventionist arrangements, forged in the 1930s and 1940s, exhibited an irresistable capacity to survive in the face of exceptionally powerful and persistent attacks upon them.

Notes

1. From Neutrality to Participation: A Prefatory Survey

1. Quoted in Walter Johnson, *The Battle Against Isolation* (New York: Da Capo Press, 1973), p. 14.

2. Thomas H. Johnson, *The Oxford Companion to American History* (New York: Oxford University Press, 1966), p. 592.

3. See Selig Adler, *The Isolationist Impulse* (New York: Free Press, 1957) p. 47.

4. *Ibid.*, p. 68.

5. See Bureau of Demobilization, Civilian Production Administration (CPA), *Industrial Mobilization for War* (Washington, D.C.: GPO, 1947), 1:73.

6. The War Resources Board reviewed the Industrial Mobilization Plan of 1930, as revised, submitted a preparedness plan to the President, and was disbanded in November 1939.

7. U.S. Congress, Senate, *Report* 480, 77th Cong., 2d sess., pt. 5, January 15, 1942.

8. Subsequently called the Manhattan Project when officially created and designated in August 1942. It was a $2 billion endeavor engaging about 125,000 employees.

9. The concept of "limited national emergency" had no constitutional sanction, but of course it had a psychological impact upon the general public.

10. $577 billion compared to $581 billion in the earlier years. These estimates are in 1972 dollars. See John C. Musgrave, "Fixed Nonresidential Business and Residential Capital in the United States, 1925–75," *Survey of Current Business*, April 1976, p. 48.

11. This is a calendar year deficit for total government in the national income and product accounts.

12. See *Survey of Current Business*, Supplement on National Income, July 1947, p. 49, table 4-3. Calculations are in current dollars.

13. John B. Rae, *Climb to Greatness: The American Aircraft Industry, 1920–1960* (Cambridge, Mass: MIT Press, 1968), pp. 132–33.

14. CPA, *Industrial Mobilization for War*, 1:187. Eliot Janeway notes with acridity the failure of Donald Nelson's *Arsenal of Democracy* to mention the Reuther plan, and the Budget Bureau's history to acknowledge the country's debt to it. See his *The Struggle for Survival* (New Haven: Yale University Press, 1951), p. 223.

15. Rae, *Climb to Greatness*, pp. 133–34.

16. CPA, *Industrial Mobilization for War*, 1:189.

17. Rae, *Climb to Greatness*, p. 157. Rae's appendixes B and C contain a complete list of firms and production of aircraft and engines, by type.

18. The highest Korean War quarterly rate for National Security outlays relative to GNP was about 15 percent, in the second quarter of 1953.

19. Geoffrey Perrett, *Days of Sadness, Years of Triumph* (Baltimore: Penguin Books, 1974), p. 211.

20. Calculated from Wladimir and Emma Woytinsky, *World Population and Production: Trends and Outlook* (New York: Twentieth Century Fund, 1953), p. 389.

21. Indexes from *Economic Report of the President*, January 1958, p. 148.

22. See U.S. Department of Commerce, *Historical Statistics of the United States, Colonial Times to 1970* (Washington, D.C.: GPO, 1975), pt. 2, p. 667. ser. P-13.

23. The percentage rise in contract construction was almost as high, but in wholesale trade the average rose only 2.4 percent, and in retail trade, reflecting long-term trends, it *fell* by 5.3 percent.

24. The armed forces totaled 458,000 in 1940, 1.8 million the next year, and 12.1 million in 1945.

25. This jump in the female participation rate was one of the more remarkable wartime phenomena. The civilian labor force also acquired many teenagers and some elderly people.

26. The data, in billions of 1947 dollars, are as follows:

	1940	1944
personal consumption outlays	122.5	135.9
gross private		
domestic investment	22.8	9.2
net foreign investment	2.2	−4.0
federal purchases,		
military commodities	2.9	87.9
	150.4	229.0

SOURCES: *Economic Report of the President*, January 1958, pp. 121–22, and *Survey of Current Business*, National Income Supplement, July 1947, pp. 19, table 2, and 27, table 14. Military commodity purchases equals all government war purchases minus military wages and salaries, a rough measure.

27. Labor hours of 102.2 billion in 1940 and 122.7 billion in 1944 are from John W. Kendrick, *Productivity Trends in the United States*, National Bureau of Economic Research (Princeton: Princeton University Press, 1961), p. 313. Although "labor productivity" is a widely used phrase, it is deceptive because it ignores the influence of other inputs and technological improvements on production. Also, in this case, rising utilization rates may have brought increasing marginal output rates.

28. *Historical Statistics*, pt. 2, p. 948, column W-5.

29. The "real value" of both the gross and the net stocks of fixed business capital fell, not only between 1940 and 1943, but throughout the war (see Musgrave, "Fixed Nonresidential Business and Residential Capital" pp. 48–49). On the other hand, Kendrick's capital input indexes for the private domestic economy rise 6 percent between 1940 and 1943 (*Productivity Trends*, p. 335).

30. Kendrick, *Productivity Trends*, p. 334–35. The index is for the private domestic economy, employing the Department of Commerce concepts of total production. Of course, the percentage increases in the twenties are from a smaller base.

31. The phase is in George A. Lincoln, *Economics of National Security* (New York: Prentice-Hall, 1954), 2d ed., p. 55.

32. ". . . Manpower is the most critical determining factor in war production today," said WPB chairman Donald M. Nelson in March 1944. See his *Arsenal of Democracy* (New York: Da Capo Press, 1973), p. 397. But elsewhere he adds, there was "never an actual over-all shortage of manpower," only "localized manpower shortages" (*ibid.*, p. 403).

33. A new series defining the labor force as persons 16 years, instead of 14 years, or older, gave the female participation rate (percent of female noninstitutional population) in 1981 as 52.1, a rise from 1946's low of 30.8. Meanwhile, the male rate had been falling, from 86.8 in 1947 to 77.0 in 1981.

34. Perrett, *Days of Sadness*, p. 259.

35. J. Steindl, "The U.S. War Effort in Terms of Man-power," Oxford University Institute of Economics and Statistics, *Labour in the War Industries of Britain and the U.S.A.*, Studies in War Economics, Bulletin (August 7, 1943), 5(11):47.

36. Sidney Pollard, *The Development of the British Economy, 1914–1950* (London: Edward Arnold, 1962), p. 327.

37. *Ibid.* Percentage calculated at market prices.

38. Calculated from *Economic Report of the President*, January 1957, pp. 123, E-1, and 133, E-10.

39. Phillis Deane and W. A. Cole, *British Economic Growth, 1688–1959* (Cambridge: Cambridge University Press, 1969), pp. 330–31. Real national income is estimated by calculating the implicit price deflators in appendix table 90, and applying same to the net national income series in that table to derive real net national income.

40. Calculated from *Economic Report of the President*, January 1957, p. 126.

41. Foreign asset liquidation helped somewhat to sustain the volume of imports, but even that index fell from 100 in 1938 to 77 in 1943 and 62 in 1945 (Pollard, *Development of the British Economy*, p. 331.)

42. John Morton Blum, "World War II," in C. Vann Woodward, ed., *The Comparative Approach to American History* (New York: Basic Books, 1968), p. 318.

43. Again, I estimate purchase of military commodities as a residual, i.e., by subtracting military wages and salaries from total federal purchases of goods and services for national defense. To get real magnitudes I use the price deflator for all federal government purchases.

44. The two sets of time periods are necessary for a proper picture because (1) 1924 was a mild recession year within the general major cycle upswing, and (2) in many if not most series 1944 had a higher level of activity than 1945. This means, of course, when using the shorter period we are comparing a peacetime year of inventory recession with the peak of wartime activity. Data source: various tables in U.S., Dept. of Commerce, *Long Term Economic Growth, 1860–1970* (Washington, D.C.: U.S. Superintendent of Documents, 1973).

45. CPA, *Industrial Mobilization for War*, 1:962.

46. Perrett, *Days of Sadness*, p. 262.

47. CPA *Industrial Mobilization for War*, 1:964.

48. *Historical Statistics*, Pt. 2, p. 893, ser. 239.

49. *Ibid.*, p. 900, ser. 302, 309.

50. U.S., Congress, Senate, Special Committe to Investigate the National Defense Program, 78th Cong., 1st sess., pt. 17, "Pipe Line Transportation," *Hearings*, February 17, 1943, pp. 6918–19.

This is the famous Senate committee under the chairmanship of Senator Harry S. Truman. It has properly been called "the most important single Congressional committee dealing with the mobilization programs of World War II," which from 1941 until 1948 covered many vital phases of that program "and exerted considerable influence on its course." Donald H. Riddle, *The Truman Committee* (New Brunswick, N.J.: Rutgers University Press, 1964), p. vii.

51. The Truman Committee in 1943 attributed the steel shortage to underestimation by the armed forces throughout 1941, as represented in the celebrated Gano Dunn report in February 1941, of steel requirements in the event of war; to the desire of the eight big steel companies to restrict capacity, together with their domination of the Iron and Steel branch of the War Production Board; and to the delay of the WPB in converting the industry to a war basis after U.S. entry. Said the committee, "untold tons of steel were permitted to be consumed in nonwar production until far into 1942." See the Committee's Interim *Report on Steel*, 78th Cong., 1st sess., Report no. 10, pt. 3, February 4, 1943, p. 2.

52. The Manhattan Project that developed the atomic bomb, as noted by Kenneth Arrow, Nobel Laureate in economics, provided a superb example of a vast and successful public enterprise conducted without reliance upon the profit motive. See Kenneth J. Arrow, "The Limitations of the Profit Motive," *Challenge* (September/October 1979), 22(4):27. Public power was vital to the success of that project.

53. David Novick, Melvin Anshen, and W. C. Truppner, *Wartime Production Controls* (New York: Columbia University Press, 1949), pp. 59, 61.

54. Richard A. Lauderbaugh, *American Steel Makers and the Coming of the Second World War* (Ann Arbor, Mich.: UMI Research Press, 1980), p. 58.

55. *Ibid.*

56. Novick, et al., *Wartime Production Controls*, p. 60.

57. Lauderbaugh, *American Steel Makers*, p. 73.

58. *Ibid.*, p. 77.

59. *Ibid.*, p. 81.

60. *Ibid.*, p. 93.

61. *Historical Statistics*, pt. 2, p. 698, ser. 302.

62. Edward L. Allen, *Economics of American Manufacturing* (New York: Henry Holt, 1952), p. 79.

63. *Historical Statistics*, pt. 1, p. 693, ser. 265.

64. *Ibid.*, p. 698, ser. 309.

65. Nelson, *Arsenal of Democracy*, p. 290.

66. *Ibid.*, pp. 292–93.

67. Cited in Allen, *Economics of Manufacturing*, p. 189.

68 U.S. Bureau of the Budget, *The United States at War* (Washington, D.C.: GPO, 1946), p. 296 n. 8.

69 U.S. Congress, Senate, Special Committee to Investigate the National Defense Program, *Additional Report*, 78th Cong., 1st sess. pt. no. 10, pt. 9, May 6 1943, pp. 1-3.

70. See Novick, et al., *Wartime Production Controls*, pp. 205–6.

71. Bureau of the Budget, *The United States at War*, p. 412, chart 49.

72. A. J. Youngson, *The British Economy, 1920–1957* (Cambridge, Mass.: Harvard University Press, 1960), p. 153. About $2 billion in additional grants were made for V-J Day through 1952; and about $0.5 billion in reverse Lend-Lease and returned Lend-Lease ships was provided. *Statistical Abstract*, 1953, p. 886, no. 1047.

73. U.S. Senate, Special Committee to Investigate the National Defense Program, *Report*, no. 10, pt. 12, November 5, 1943, p. 13.

74. Pollard, *Development of the British Economy*, p. 337.

75 *Ibid.* The following sentence is also quoted from *ibid.*, pp. 337–38.

2. Administration in the Preparedness Period

1. See, e.g., U.S. Civilian Production Administration (CPA), Bureau of Demobilization, *Minutes of the Advisory Commission to the Council of National Defense*, Historical Reports on War Administration, War Production Board, Documentary Publication no. 1 (Washington, D.C.: GPO, 1946), pp. 72–73, 81, 88–90.

2. *Ibid.*, p. 93.

3. U.S., CPA, Bureau of Demobilization, *Minutes of the Council of the Office of Production Management*, Historical Reports on War Administration, War Production Board, Documentary Publication no. 2 (Washington, D.C.: GPO, 1946), pp. iii, 1.

4. Richard J. Purcell, *Labor Policies of the National Defense Advisory Commission and the Office of Production Management, May 1940 to April 1942*, Historical Reports on War Administration, War Production Board (Washington, D.C.: Civilian Production Administration, October 31, 1946), p. 19.

5. *Ibid.*, p. 27.

6. Eliot Janeway, *The Struggle for Survival* (New Haven: Yale University Press, 1951), p. 201.

7. *Ibid.*, p. 203.

8. Joan Mitchell, *Groundwork to Economic Planning* (London: Secker and Warburg, 1966), pp. 56–57.

9. Walter W. Wilcox, *The Farmer in the Second World War* (Ames: Iowa State College Press, 1947), pp. 38–39; and Bela Gold, *Wartime Economic Planning in Agriculture* (New York: AMS Press, 1968), p. 23.

10. David Novick, Melvin Anshen, and W. C. Truppner, *Wartime Production Controls* (New York: Columbia University Press, 1949), pp. 370–71.

11. *Ibid.*, p. 77.

12. Drummond Jones, *The Role of the Office of Civilian Requirements in the Office of Production Management and War Production Board*, Historical Reports on War Administration, War Production Board (Washington, D.C.: Civilian Production Administration, May 15, 1946), pp. 10–12.

13. *Ibid.*, p. 22.

14. *Ibid.*, p. 35.

15. Cited in *ibid.*, p. 36.

16. With regard to this clash over jurisdiction see the OPM Council's *Minutes* for June 10, 1941; July 1, 1941; and July 22, 1941; CPA, *Minutes of the Council*, pp. 31, 36–37, 45.

17. See U.S. Bureau of the Budget, *The United States at War* (Washington, D.C.: GPO, 1946), pp. 173–75.

18. Purcell, *Labor Policies*, p. 41, table 1.

19. *Ibid.*, pp. 128, 132.

20. *Ibid.*, p. 178.

21. *Ibid.*, p. 9.

22. *Ibid.*, p. 216.

23. *Ibid.*, p. 220.

24. *Ibid.*, pp. 228–29.

25. *Ibid.*, p. 235.

26. See the five-point plan for labor protection growing out of a meeting on the rubber crisis held in Akron, Ohio, in December 1941; Purcell, *Labor Policies*, pp. 142–43.

27. At the May 13, 1941, meeting of the OPM Council, these developments were noted by Hillman, and the council agreed (1) the wage problem needed to be studied, and (2) the government needed a fair general wage policy! See CPA, *Minutes of the Council*, p. 21.

28. Purcell, *Labor Policies*, p. 171.

29. *Ibid.*, p. 46.

30. *Ibid.*, pp. 48, 56, 57–58.

31. *Ibid.*, p. 5.

32. *Ibid.*, p. 64.

33. *Ibid.*, p. 190.

34. See Gold, *Wartime Economic Planning in Agriculture*, pp. 282–83. It is not to be inferred that Gold evaluates the department's wartime direction as first class—far from it.

35. Howard R. Smith, *Government and Business* (New York: Ronald Press, 1958), pp. 539–40.

36. Wilcox, *The Farmer in the Second World War*, pp. 374–75.

37. Davis had been Advisor on Farm Products on the NDAC, a function absorbed, beginning May 5, 1941, by the Office of Agricultural Defense Relations.

38. Wilcox, *The Farmer in the Second World War*, p. 352.

3. Two Studies in Wartime Business: Farming and Small Enterprise

1. For a detailed, scholarly survey of the war experience see Walter Wilcox, *The Farmer in the Second World War* (Ames: Iowa State College Press, 1947).

2. Cited in Eliot Janeway, *The Struggle for Survival* (New Haven: Yale University Press, 1951).

3. U.S. Bureau of the Budget, *The United States at War* (Washington, D.C.: GPO, 1946), p. 321.

4. Data in *Historical Statistics*, pt. 1, pp. 469, 827, 830 show that tractors on farms rose steadily from 1,567,000 in 1940 to 2,354,000 in 1945; motor trucks by 42 percent; grain combines by 97 percent; corn pickers by 53 percent; commercial fertilizer consumed by 62 percent; and lime consumed on farms by 60 percent. The proportion of farm dwellings with electric service rose from a third to almost a half, and electric energy purchased from the Rural Electrification Administration increased by 437 percent. However, the farm operators disposed of horses and mules at rates that were without precedent. Alvin S. Tostlebe, *The Growth of Physical Capital in Agriculture, 1870–1950*, Occasional Paper 44 (New York: National Bureau of Economic Research, 1954), pp. 50–51.

5. Wilcox, *The Farmer in the Second World War*, p. 56.

6. Theodore W. Schultz, *Agriculture in an Unstable Economy* (New York: McGraw-Hill, 1945), p. 26.

7. U.S. Congress, Senate, Special Committee to Investigate the National Defense Program, 78th Cong., 1st sess., *Interim Report on Farm Machinery and Equipment*, Report no. 10, pt. 2, January 21, 1943, pp. 9–19, *passim*.

8. *Ibid*. Professor Bela Gold, who worked in the Bureau of Agricultural Economics during the war, charged in his *Wartime Planning in Agriculture* (New York: AMS Press, 1968) that despite self-laudatory statements by both federal officials and farm spokesmen, the truth was that the federal government failed to provide effective leadership to mobilize agriculture (e.g., pp. 497–98, 512, 530, 542–43).

9. John W. Kendrick, *Productivity Trends in the United States*, Natural Bureau of Economic Research (Princeton: Princeton University Press, 1969), p. 364, table B-1. Estimating total capital (including land) input to have been about constant from 1942 through 1945, with net output as estimated by Kendrick falling somewhat, there was a fall in net output per unit of capital input.

10. The first so-called golden age was 1910–14. The indexes are from *Historical Statistics*, pt. 1, p. 489, ser. 344, 352, 353. Comparison with wholesale prices of farm products in chart 5.1 (on a different base) may be of interest.

11. Geoffrey H. Moore, "Secular Changes in the Distribution of Income," *American Economic Review* (May 1952), 42(2):541 and n. 9.

12. *Economic Report of the President*, January 1956, p. 135.

13. The quinquennial percentage declines after the war were: 1945–50, 4; 1950–55, 18; 1955–60, 15; 1960–65, 15; 1965–70, 12; 1970–75, 6; 1975–80, 4. Data from *Statistical Abstract*, 1977, p. 674, no. 1134, and 1982–83, p. 652, no. 1140.

14. The South's farm population was 54 percent of the U.S. total in 1940, but its decline during the war accounted for 60 percent of the aggregate fall for the nation.

15. See Sidney Pollard, *The Development of the British Economy, 1914–1950* (London: Edward Arnold, 1962), pp. 314–16.

16. Data from *Historical Statistics*, pt. 2, ser. V-13, p. 911, and ser. V-40, p. 914. Estimates of the business population are notoriously crude.

17. *Historical Statistics*, pt. 2, ser. V-23, p. 912.

18. Corporate income is receipts less deductions (*ibid.*, p. 924–25, ser. V-108–40). The corporate universe here is all corporations which (1) filed income tax returns to the U.S. Internal Revenue Service, and also (2) supplied balance sheet information.

19. U.S., Smaller War Plants Corporation, *Program and Progress Report*, Eleventh Bimonthly Report, May 1, 1944 (Washington, D.C.: GPO, 1944), p. 4.

20. Donald M. Nelson, *Arsenal of Democracy* (New York: Da Capo Press, 1973), pp. 177, 198.

21. *Ibid.*, p. 163.

22. *Ibid.*, pp. 163–64.

23. *Ibid.*, p. 279. The WPB was nominally given major powers to direct military procurement and war production, including authority to issue all priority ratings. Nelson remained chairman until his feud with the services forced his resignation in September 1944, and he was replaced by New Dealer J. A. Krug, formerly manager of power for the Tennessee Valley Authority.

24. Robert Wood Johnson, *"But, General Johnson"* (Princeton: Princeton University Press, 1941), p. 6. The immediately following account relies heavily upon Johnson's work.

25. See Jim F. Heath, "American War Mobilization and the Use of Small Manufacturers, 1939–1943," *Business History Review* (Autumn 1972), 46(3):306–7, 314.

26. Johnson, *"But, General Johnson,"* p. 9.

27. *Ibid.*, p. 8.

28. *Ibid.* Of course, not all small firms or plants possessed facilities or personnel adaptable to the *ordnance* program.

29. Actually, the act established both the SWPC and a Smaller War Plants Division of the WPB. While these were separate agencies, Nelson attempted to bridge *the* separation by appointing Lou E. Holland as both head of the division and chairman of SWPC. General Robert W. Johnson was appointed new deputy chairman of the division in February 1943, and the next month the division was replaced by the SWPC. Johnson remained until replaced by Maury Maverick on January 19, 1944.

30. Nelson, *Arsenal of Democracy*, p. 384.

31. Bureau of the Budget, *The United States at War*, p. 312.

32. Nelson, *Arsenal of Democracy*, p. 270.

33. Johnson, *"But General Johnson,"* p. 17.

34. U.S., Smaller War Plants Corporation (SWPC) *Economic Concentration and World War II*. Report of the Smaller War Plants Corporation to the Senate Special Committee to Study the Problems of American Small Business, Senate Doc. no. 206, 79th Cong., 2d sess. Senate Committee Print no. 6 (Washington, D.C.: GPO, 1946), p. 29.

35. *Ibid.*, p. 32. Note the exclusive reference to *corporations*.

36. U.S., Senate, Special Commitee to Investigate the National Defense Program, *Third Annual Report*, 78th Cong., 2d sess, rpt. no. 10, pt. 16, March 4, 1944, p. 14.

37. SWPC, *Report to Congress*, Twentieth Bimonthly Report, August and September 1945, p. 32, table.

38. *Historical Statistics*, pt. 2, p. 911, ser. V 15.

39. SWPC, *Economic Concentration and World War II*, pp. 311, 315. On the other hand, the *Survey of Current Business, National Income Supplement* for 1951 (pp. 186–87) lists 124,000 "active proprietors of unincorporated" manufacturing firms in 1939 and 157,000 in 1944, a 27 percent rise. This surprising increase in overwhelmingly small manufacturers is offset, however, by an equally surprising decline of 9,000 manufacturing corporations (*Historical Statistics*, pt. 2, p. 914). The total of the two legal forms of organization shows an 11.4 percent rise.

40. SWPC, *Economic Concentration and World War II*, pp. 314, table B-3 and 318, table B-4.

41. *Ibid.*

42. See Harold G. Vatter, "The Position of Small Business in the Structure of American Manufacturing 1870–1970," in Stuart W. Bruchey, ed., *Small Business in American Life* (New York: Columbia University Press, 1980), pp. 154–55.

43. The SWPC, in its Eleventh Bimonthly Report (*Program and Progress Report*, p. 3) cited the Truman Committee as having estimated that military orders on hand in representative large corporations averaged 14 months' production; medium-sized firms, 8 months' production; small manufacturers, a 5-month backlog. For the small firm with a military contract this situation as the war was approaching its end was potentially two-sided: it would lose its contract sooner, but, if it could get materials and labor and restock where necessary, it might get into the civilian market earlier than its larger competitors—assuming it had an independent market potential apart from supplying some large buyer that was still producing ordnance.

44. Harold Stein, ed., *Public Administration and Policy Development* (New York: Harcourt, Brace, 1952), p. 235. The discussion in this work on "The Reconversion Controversy," written by Jack W. Peltason (pp. 215–83), is an invaluable survey of the subject.

45. In the War Department's official history, for example, there appears, inter alia, the following remark: "But there was one feature of the Small Business Act which Army procurement officials considered above all others to be gratuitous and positively dangerous to the success of the procurement program. This was the provision for the Smaller War Plants Corporation to take prime contracts for military procurement following certification by the WPB chairman. To Army procurement officials this appeared as a device to set up a dual procurement agency and to take the procurement function out of the hands of the War Department." R. Elberton Smith, *The Army and Economic Mobilization*, War Department, Office of the Chief of Military History, Department of the Army (Washington, D.C.: GPO, 1959), p. 426.

46. *Ibid.*, p. 696, table 60.

47. Stein, *Public Administration*, pp. 239–40; Barton J. Bernstein, "The Debate on Industrial Reconversion," *American Journal of Economics and Sociology* (1967), 26:166; and *Business Week* for June 17, 1944, July 1, 1944, and December 30, 1944. It is of some journalistic interest that *Business Week* failed to report the events in the Brewster story between the time of its statement on July 1 that the corporation was "reconverting . . . for production of civilian goods" and its story on the auction in its December 30 issue.

48. Stein, *Public Administration*, p. 266.

49. *Ibid.*, pp. 266–67.

50. Cited in Bernstein, "Debate on Industrial Reconversion," p. 167.

51. Cited in Stein, *Public Administration*, p. 270.

52. *Ibid.*, pp. 268–69. See also Bernstein, "Debate on Industrial Reconversion," p. 168.

53. Bernstein, *ibid.*, p. 172, concludes that PR 25 may have saved a few hundred marginal firms.

54. A. D. H. Kaplan, *The Liquidation of War Production* (New York: McGraw-Hill, 1944), p. 89. Kaplan asks rhetorically, why did the government not leave the financing of war plant facilities to private capital, as was done in 1917? His aswer is that "private capital investment is necessarily limited by the prospects of future returns. Obviously, on an investment basis, private capital could not provide enough facilities with which to wage a global war" (p. 92).

55. John D. Sumner, "The Disposition of Surplus War Property," *American Economic Review* (September 1944), 34(1):457.

56. SWPC, *Economic Concentration and World War II*, p. 48.

57. *Ibid.*, p. 49. The federally financed expansion consisted chiefly of tremendous plants which only government or large corporations could profitably operate after the necessary adaptation, in peacetime. Only $250 million of the $12 billion authorized for new plants was for units costing less than $1 million apiece: 816 plants. See U.S., Civilian Production Administration, Industrial Statistics Division, *War-Created Manufacturing Plant Federally Financed, 1940–1944* (November 15, 1945), p. 3.

58. John D. Sumner, "Disposition of Surplus War Property," p. 463.

59. The location, ownership, and capacity of all aluminum reduction plants in the United States in 1944 may be found in U.S. Tariff Commission, *Aluminum*, War Changes in Industry Series, Report no. 14 (Washington, D.C.: GPO, 1946), p. 76, table 19.

60. William N. Leonard, *Business Size, Market Power, and Public Policy* (New York: Thomas Y. Crowell, 1969), p. 52.

61. Barton J. Bernstein, "The Removal of War Production Board Controls on Business, 1944–46," *Business History Review* (1965), 39:251, 253. Construction materials were especially scarce, and Bowles' prediction that decontrols would aggravate new housing price inflation was strongly borne out by subsequent developments.

62. *Ibid.*, p. 258.

63. *Ibid.*, p. 255.

64. *Ibid.*, p. 260.

65. See U.S., Bureau of the Census, *Census of Manufactures*, 1958, 1:2-2; *Statistical Abstract*, 1975, p. 736 no. 1260, and p. 741, no. 1263.

66. The number of single-unit companies, in contrast to multiunit firms, stopped increasing between 1954 and 1972. However, there were 279,000 five years later. (*Statistical Abstract*, 1979, p. 800, no. 1413; and 1982–83, p. 768, no. 1378. The manufacturing deflator used is from U.S., Department of Commerce, Bureau of Economic Analysis, *The National Income and Product Accounts of the United States, 1929–1974* (Washington, D.C.: GPO, 1977), p. 296, table 7-15).

4. Wartime Administration

1. Cited and discussed in Drummond Jones, *The Role of the Office of Civilian Requirements in the Office of Production Management and War Production Board, January 1941 to November 1945*, Historical Reports on War Administration, War Production Board, Special Study no. 20, Civilian Production Administration (Washington, D.C., May 15, 1946), p. 209. See also p. 131. Nelson made the statement in April 1943.

2. U.S., Civilian Production Administration (CPA), Bureau of Demobilization, *Industrial Mobilization for War* (Washington, D.C.: Civilian Products Administration, 1947), 1:18.

3. Herman Miles Somers, *Presidential Agency OWMR* (New York: Greenwood Press, 1969), p. 43.

4. Richard J. Purcell, *Labor Policies of the National Defense Advisory Commission and the Office of Production Management, May 1940 to April 1942*, Historical Reports on War Administration, War Production Board (Washington, D.C.: Civilian Production Administration, October 31, 1946), pp. 30–33.

5. Selective Service was blanketed under WMC in December 1942, but Congress jerked it out at the end of 1943 because "the selection of men for the military service was never part of a long-range and comprehensive manpower program." Quoted from the Budget Bureau history by Eliot Janeway, *The Struggle for Survival* (New Haven: Yale University Press, 1951), p. 326.

6. Bureau of Demobilization, Civilian Production Administration, (CPA), *Industrial Mobilization for War* (Washington, D.C.: GPO, 1947), 1:559.

7. *Ibid.*, p. 562.

8. *Ibid.*, p. 568–69.

9. Cited in CPA, *Industrial Mobilization for War*, 1:213.

10. U.S. Bureau of the Budget, *The United States at War* (Washington, D.C.: GPO, 1946), p. 380.

11. See the appraisal by John D. Millett, *The Process and Organization of Government Planning* (New York: Columbia University Press, 1947), p. 97.

12. Bureau of the Budget, *The United States at War*, pp. 113–14. The citation is rearranged and emphasized by Janeway, *Struggle for Survival*, pp. 308–9.

13. U.S., CPA, *Minutes of the WPB*, January 26, 1943, p. 189.

14. Jones, *Role of the OCR*, pp. 59, 79.

15. *Ibid.*, pp. 63, 65.

16. *Ibid.*, p. 96.

17. CPA, *Industrial Mobilization for War*, 1:619.

18. Jones, *Role of the OCR*, foreword.

19. *Ibid.*, pp. 108, 111.

20. Cited in *ibid.*, p. 112.

21. David Novick, Melvin Anshen, and W. C. Truppner, *Wartime Production Controls* (New York: Columbia University Press, 1949), p. 105.

22. *Ibid.*, p. 165.

23. *Ibid.*, pp. 171–72.

24. CPA, *Industrial Mobilization for War*, 1:632.

25. See Harry A. Millis and Royal E. Montgomery, *Organized Labor* (New York: McGraw-Hill, 1945), pp. 769–71, *passim*.

26. *Ibid.*, p. 772.

27. Cited in Philip Taft, *Organized Labor in American History* (New York: Harper and Row, 1964), p. 560.

28. CPA, *Industrial Mobilization for War*, 1:423.

29. Cited in Sanford M. Jacoby, "Union-Management Cooperation in the United States During World War II," in Melvyn Dubovsky, ed., *Technological Change and Worker Movements in the Modern World* (Beverly Hills: Sage Press, 1985).

30. *Ibid.* What follows immediately relies heavily upon Jacoby.

31. CPA, *Industrial Mobilization for War*, 1:554.

32. *Ibid.*

33. Janeway, *Struggle for Survival*, p. 16.

34. Cited in Somers, *Presidential Agency OWMR*, p. 47. The following discussion of OWM draws heavily upon Somers' incisive presentation.

35. *Ibid.*

36. CPA, *Industrial Mobilization for War*, 1:721.

37. *Ibid.*, 1:721.

38. *Ibid.*, 1:721–22.

39. Somers, *Presidential Agency OWMR*, p. 59.

40. *Ibid.*, p. 64.

41. J. Donald Kingsley, "Top-Level Coordination of Wartime Programs," paper delivered in the *Public Administration Lecture Series*, U.S. Dept of Agriculture Graduate School, October 1, 1946. Cited in Somers, *Presidential Agency OWMR*, p. 205n.

42. Janeway, *Struggle for Survival*, p. 359.

43. Millett, *Process and Organization*, p. 159.

44. See Bernard M. Baruch and John M. Hancock, *Report on War and Post-War Adjustment Policy*, S. Doc. no. 154, 78th Cong., 2d sess., February 1944. The *Report* urged that "The demobilization or unwinding of our war economy can best be done by the same agencies which wound up our industrial mobilization . . ." (p. 69). The study leading to the *Report* was under Hancock's direction.

45. See *Reconversion*, Report to the President from the Director of War Mobilization, September 7, 1944, esp. pp. 11–12. In the *Second Report* (April 1, 1945) of the Director of OWMR it was reported that OPA had "worked out" such a "program of resumption of prices" (p. 23). See the summary of WPB reconversion preparations in CPA, *Minutes* of the WPB, October 9, 1945.

46. Cited in CPA, *Industrial Mobilization for War*, 1:575.

47. Jack W. Peltason, *The Reconversion Controversy*, Committee on Public Administration Cases (New York: Bobbs-Merrill, 1950), p. 139.

48. William Haber, "Man Power and Reconversion," in Seymour E. Harris, *ed., Economic Reconstruction* (New York: McGraw-Hill, 1946), p. 105.

49. For an excellent and extensive tabulation of where the wartime administration stood on reconversion as of September 1945, see U.S., Office of War Mobilization and Reconversion, *Fourth Report* (Washington, D.C., October 1, 1945).

50. The WLB went into the Labor Department in September 1945.

51. See CPA, *Industrial Mobilization for War*, 1:868.

52. Cited in *ibid.*, p. 945.

5.   Stabilization and the Office of Price Administration

1. U.S., Civilian Production Administration, *Minutes* of the WPB, December 8, 1942, p. 171.

2. Emmette S. Redford, *Field Administration of Wartime Rationing*, Office of Temporary Controls, Historical Reports on War Administration, no. 4 (Washington, D.C.: GPO, May 1947), p. 9.

3. *Ibid.*, pp. 23, 24, 182.

4. Victor A. Thompson, *The Regulatory Process in OPA Rationing* (New York: King's Crown and Columbia University Press, 1950), pp. 33-34.

5. *Ibid.*, pp. 36-39, *passim*.

6. Based upon 1947–49 average equals 100. The consumer price index is for average city wage-earner and clerical worker families. Source: *Economic Report of the President*, January 1957, pp. 160, 164. It seems likely that the greater farm price rise was in part a correction for the severe imbalances during the Great Depression. The implicit price deflator for personal consumption expenditures on a 1947 base rose 11 percent in 1942 over 1941 (*ibid.*, p. 128).

7. U. S. Bureau of the Budget, *The United States at War* (Washington, D.C.: GPO, 1946), p. 235.

8. John Kenneth Galbraith, *A Theory of Price Control* (Cambridge: Harvard University Press, 1952).

9. *Ibid.*, p. 14.

10. *Ibid.*, p. 21.

11. *Ibid.*, Introduction to the 1980 edition.

12. Imogene H. Putnam, *Volunteers in OPA*, Office of Temporary Controls, Office of Price Administration, Historical Reports on War Administration, Publication no. 14 (Washington, D.C.: GPO, May 1947).

13. *Ibid.*, p. 28.

14. *Ibid.* There could also have been other ideological influences at work, e.g., an assumption that (*a*) there was enough slack to dampen price increases, and/or (*b*) some price increase was healthy because it would reduce civilian consumption.

15. Galbraith, *Theory of Price Control*, p. 15.

16. Galbraith argues that in a competive market "the initiative to violation of a price regulation is . . . as likely to be assumed by the buyer as by the seller." *Ibid.*, p. 14.

17. Putnam, *Volunteers in OPA*, p. 28.

18. *Ibid.*, pp. 28–29.

19. Cited in *ibid.*, p. 29.

20. *Ibid.*, pp. 29–30.

21. *Ibid.*, pp. 30–31.

22. *Ibid.*, pp. 31–32.

23. *Ibid.*, p. 32.

24. *Ibid.*, p. 37.

25. Cited in Bureau of the Budget, *The United States at War*, p. 383.

26. See Walter W. Wilcox and Willard W. Cochrane, *Economics of American Agriculture* (Englewood Cliffs, N.J.: Prentice-Hall, 1960), p. 473.

27. Bela Gold, *Wartime Economic Planning in Agriculture* (New York: AMS Press, 1968), pp. 406–7 and table 50.

28. See Sol A. Segal, "Basic Legislative Standards for Agricultural Commodities," in James B. Echkert, ed., *Problems in Price Control: Pricing Standards*, Office of Temporary Controls, Historical Reports on War Administration (Washington, D.C.: GPO, May 1947), p. 171.

29. See Seymour Harris, "Stabilization Subsidies, 1942–1946," in *Problems in Price Control: Stabilization Subsidies*, Office of Price Administration and Office of Temporary Controls (Washington: D.C.: GPO, May 1947), pp. 40–45, *passim.*

30. *Economic Report of the President*, January 1957, p. 164.

31. See Wilfred Carsel, "Wartime Apparel Price Control," U.S. Office of Temporary Controls, OPA, Historical Reports on War Administration, General Publication no. 3 (Washington, D.C.: GPO, April 1947), pp. 7, 103–4, 106–7, 109.

32. *Ibid.*, pp. vii, 132.

33. *Ibid.*, p. 375. See also pp. 379 and 431 n. 15.

34. Regarding labor's preference on this matter in 1942, see Philip Taft, *Organized Labor in American History* (New York: Harper and Row, 1964), pp. 548–49.

35. Hugh Rockoff, "Indirect Price Increases and Real Wages During World War II," *Explorations in Economic History* (October 1978), 15(4):407–20.

36. Hugh Rockoff, *Money: Whence It Came, Where It Went* (Boston: Houghton Mifflin, 1975), pp. 242–43. Galbraith's price index base year is 1967.

37. Milton Friedman and Anna Jacobson Schwartz, *A Monetary History of the United States, 1867–1960* (Princeton University Press, 1963), p. 558.

38. *Ibid.*, p. 558.

39. These periods are taken from *ibid.*, p. 548, column headings for table 23.

40. Rockoff, *Money*, p. 417, table 4.

41. *Monthly Labor Review*, August 1946, p. 259. Cited in Rockoff, "Indirect Price Increase."

42. Data from Friedman and Schwartz, *Monetary History*, pp. 716–17, table A-1.

43. See *Economic Report of the President*, January 1951, p. 51, table 1.

44. The consumer price index was also stable from 1948 to 1950.

45. "Discussion," in "The Role of War in American Economic Development," *American Economic Review*, (May 1952), 42(2):642.

46. Incidentally, money wage rates also rose sharply after 1945. Comparison of the average hourly wage rate for manufacturing production workers with the consumer price index (1947–49 = 100) is:

	Wage rate	CPI
1945	1.02	76.9
1946	1.08	83.4
1947	1.22	95.5
1948	1.33	102.8

The CPI on the base 1967 = 100 was:

1945	53.9
1946	58.5
1947	66.9
1948	72.1

6. Federal Fiscal and Monetary Policy

1. See "How to Pay for the War," in *The Collected Writings of* John Maynard Keynes, vol. 4, *Essays in Persuasion* (London: Macmillan, 1972), pp. 367–439.

2. As Milton Friedman properly once commented, "estimating the gap is a presumptuous undertaking." "Discussion of the Inflationary Gap," *Essays in Positive Economics* (Chicago: University of Chicago Press, 1953), p. 261).

3. As Friedman comments, "closing the gap by inflation" is an analytical trap, for when prices rise so do incomes (*ibid.*, pp. 252–53). However, these are *ex post* magnitudes, and the income effects of the price rises are contained in the personal income data. See the discussion of "total income gap" and "disposable consumer income gap" in Walter Salant, "The Inflationary Gap," *American Economic Review* (June 1942), 36(2):310–11.

4. Milton Friedman and Anna Jacobson Schwartz, A *Monetary History of the United States, 1867–1960* (Princeton: Princeton University Press, 1963), p. 568.

5. Paul Studenski and Herman E. Krooss, *Financial History of the United States* (New York: McGraw-Hill, 1963), p. 454.

6. The increase in nominal M_2 was 106 percent from August 1941 to August 1945; if deflated by the 1935–39 based CPI, the real M_2 rose 68 percent.

7. Studenski and Kroos comment on "the failure of individual subscriptions to equal expectations . . . they barely achieved their goal or fell short of it, whereas other nonbank investors . . . far exceeded their goal in every case" (*Financial History*, p. 454).

8. This statement is based on the average of the annual M_2 increases, divided by the annual differences between disposable personal money income and actual current dollar personal consumption expenditures, 1941–45. A sharper perspective emerges by comparison of the average annual increase of 8 percent in M, with the approximately 3 percent increase in the real flow of civilian goods.

9. Studenski and Krooss, *Financial History*, pp. 442–43.

10. Of the federal debt increase of $230 billion between June 1940 and December 1945, nearly $75 billion was taken by commercial banks ($22 billion by the Federal Reserve Banks). See Lester V. Chandler, "Federal Reserve Policy and the Federal Debt," *American Economic Review* (March 1949), 39(2):408.

11. In this connection see the summary of Federal Reserve wartime policy in Chandler, "Federal Reserve Policy," pp. 407–11.

7. Wartime Social Changes

1. The percentage rise in the female labor force participation rate, by decade, has been:

1940–50	12.2%
1949–59	11.5
1959–69	11.5
1969–79	11.9

Economic Report of the President, January 1979, p. 214.

The hump from 1940 to 1945 (chapter 1) was dissipated after the war, so that these figures show a steady, long-run rise rather than a sharp jump.

2. These percentages are based upon estimates in the *Statistical Abstract*, 1953, pp. 14 and 17, nos. 9 and 10.

3. William Haber, "Man Power and Reconversion," in Seymour E. Harris, ed., *Economic Reconstruction* (New York: MacGraw-Hill, 1946), p. 102.

4. Why is the 1939 rate about the same as 1925? Because couples behaved as if the economic cycle was in a buoyant phase—as in a sense it was, compared with the early years of the 1930s. The average marriage rate during 1930–33 was 8.6 per thousand.

5. See William F. Ogburn, "Marriages, Births, and Divorces: *The American Family in World War II*," *The Annals* (Philadelphia: American Academy of Political and Social Science, 1943), p. 28.

6. This relation between the marriage rate and the birth rate was short run. In the very long run the ratio of the birth rate per 1,000 to the marriage rate per 1,000 has fallen dramatically, e.g., from 2.92 in 1910 to about 1.50 in the late 1970s.

7. *Historical Statistics*, p. 41, ser. 310. The number of married couples in households, which hardly increased at all from 1940 to 1945, rose by 10.9 million between 1945 and 1957, whereas in the next twelve years of "baby bust" it was to rise by only 6.8 million.

8. See William P. Butz and Michael P. Ward, "The Emergence of Countercyclical U.S. Fertility," *American Economic Review* (June 1979), 69(3):318–27. These writers argue that the baby bust of the 1960s was due primarily to increase in women's wages and income (pp. 318, 323). Expenditures for veterans' programs jumped from a little over $1 billion in 1945 to around $5–6 billion in the early fifties.

9. Richard Easterlin, "The American Baby Boom in Historical Perspective," *American Economic Review* (December 1961), 51(5):897. On these points Easterlin cites W. H. Grabill, C. V. Kiser, and P. K. Whelpton, *The Fertility of American Women* (New York: Wiley, 1958).

10. Richard Easterlin, "Economic-Demographic Interactions and Long Swings in Economic Growth," *American Economic Review* (December 1966), 51(5):1082–85; and Richard A. Easterlin, Michael L. Wachter, and Susan M. Wachter, "Here Comes Another Baby Boom," *The Wharton Magazine* (Summer 1979), 4(3):29–33.

11. See Harold G. Vatter, *The U.S. Economy in the 1950s* (New York: Norton, 1963), pp. 8-10. The average U.S. family size rose throughout the 1950s, plateaued in the first half of the 1960s, then fell. The baby boom affected the timing of arrival of children but apparently had little effect upon completed family size in the longer period. See comments of Bernard Okun on Gary S. Becker, "An Economic Analysis of Fertility," in *Demographic and Economic Change in Developed Countries*, National Bureau of Economic Research (Princeton: Princeton University Press, 1960), p. 239.

12. All calculations on labor force participation are from the *Statistical Abstract*, 1980, p. 398, no. 658.

13. Stanley Lebergott, "Population Change and the Supply of Labor," in NBER, *Demographic and Economic Change, p. 377.*

14. John R. Craf, *A Survey of the American Economy, 1940–1946* (New York: North River Press, 1947).

15. See Joseph G. Rayback, *A History of American Labor* (New York: Macmillan, 1959), pp. 376, 380.

16. However, the subsequent spread of portal-to-portal pay was severely restricted by the federal Portal-to-Portal Act of 1947, especially for unorganized workers without contracts.

17. See the statements of John L. Lewis quoted in Philip Taft, *Organized Labor in American History* (New York: Harper and Row, 1964), pp. 552, 554.

18. See John L. Blackman, Jr., *Presidential Seizure in Labor Disputes* (Cambridge, Mass.: Harvard University Press, 1967), Appendix A, pp. 261-75.

19. Taft, *Organized Labor*, p. 557; and also, e.g., Rayback, *History of American Labor*, pp. 381–82.

20. Blackman, *Presidential Seizure*, pp. 263–78, *passim*. The seizures continued after the war's end, the last one being on June 14, 1946.

21. See J. David Greenstone, *Labor in American Politics* (New York: Random House and Knopf, 1969), pp. 6–10 *passim*.

22. *Ibid.*, pp. 50–51.

23. "The conference demonstrated for the first time in history that at a national level representatives from both labor and management could meet together without arguing as to whether or not collective bargaining was desirable." Arthur F. McClure, *The Truman Administration and the Problems of Postwar Labor, 1945–1948* (Cranbury, N.J.: Associated University Presses, 1969), p. 63. All the participants agreed in advance to limit the agenda to matters concerning industrial disputes.

24. Tuskegee Institute, Department of Records and Research, *Negro Year Book*, 1947, p. 134.

25. Bernard Sternsher, ed., *The Negro in Depression and War* (Chicago: Quadrangle Books, 1969), pp. 310–11.

26. Statement of James D. Tarver in U.S., Senate Committee on Government Operations, Subcommittee on Government Research, *The Rural to Urban Population Shift: A National Problem*, 90th Cong., 2d sess. (Washington, D.C.: GPO, 1968), p. 19, table 1.

27. *Ibid.*, p. 20, table 2.

28. *Ibid.*, p. 21, table 3.

29. Elton Rayack, "Discrimination and the Occupational Progress of Negroes," *Review of Economics and Statistics* (May 1961), 43(2);213, table 8.

30. *Ibid.*, p. 213, table 7.

31. Data upon which this statement and the immediately following estimates and calculations are based may be found in Everett S. Lee, Ann Ratner Miller, Carol P. Brainerd, and Richard A. Easterlin, *Population Redistribution and Economic Growth, United States, 1870–1950* (Philadelphia: American Philosophical Society, 1957), reference table P-1, 1:107-231.

32. John Kenneth Galbraith, *The Nature of Mass Poverty* (Cambridge, Mass.: Harvard University Press, 1979), pp. 131–32.

33. These and the immediately following calculations for 1940 and 1944 are drawn from Seymour L. Wolfbein, "War and Post-War Trends in Employment of Negroes," *Monthly Labor Review* (January 1945), 60:104. Data for later years are from U.S., Department of Labor, *Handbook of Labor Statistics*, 1972, p. 62.

34. *Negro Year Book*, 1947, p. 140.

35. *Monthly Labor Review*, January 1945, p. 3.

36. *Negro Year Book*, 1947, pp. 140–41. Not many were craftsmen or craftswomen.

37. Richard Polenberg, *War and Society: The United States, 1941–1945* (Philadelphia: J. B. Lippincott, 1972), p. 124.

38. *Ibid.*

39. Blacks had to submit to the sight of Nazi POWs eating with white GIs and civilians in dining cars and restaurants while they were barred. Charles E. Silberman, *Crisis in Black and White* (New York: Random House, 1964), p. 60.

40. *The Negro Almanac* (New York: Bellwether, 1967), p. 551. In actuality, as distinguished from officially, segregation ended under the battle pressures of the Korean War.

41. Polenberg, *War and Society*, p. 117.

42. Silberman, *Crisis in Black and White*, p. 65.

43. John E. Means, "Fair Employment Practices Legislation and Enforcement in the United States," in Louis A. Ferman, Joyce K. Kornbluh, and J. A. Miller, eds., *Negroes and Jobs* (Ann Arbor: University of Michigan Press, 1968), p. 467.

44. *Negro Year Book*, 1947, p. 350.

45. Robert C. Weaver, *Negro Labor: A National Problem* (Port Washington, N.Y.: Kennikat Press, 1946), pp. 88–89.

46. U.S., Dept. of Labor, War Manpower Commission, *Utilization of Reserve Workers, Recently Reported Placement of Negroes in Skilled Occupations* (Washington, D.C., March 1944), p. 4.

47. Weaver, *Negro Labor*, p. 89.

48. F. Ray Marshall, *The Negro Worker* (New York: Random House, 1967), p. 96, table 6.2; and Joe L. Russell, "Changing Patterns of Employment of Nonwhite Workers," in Ferman et al., *Negroes and Jobs*, p. 99, table 1. Note that the data refer to "nonwhites," not blacks.

49. Weaver, *Negro Labor*, p. 90.

50. Russell, "Changing Patterns."

51. Portland *Oregonian*, July 24, 1978, reporting a speech and subsequent interview at a JACL banquet. It was "understandable" that German and Italian Americans were not corralled only because they were more dispersed, hard to identify, and much more politically influential.

52. Dillon S. Myer, *Uprooted Americans* (Tucson: University of Arizona Press, 1971), p. 254.

53. *Ibid.*, pp. 255, 248.

54. *Ibid.*, p. 255.

55. Keith W. Olson, *The G.I. Bill, the Veterans, and the Colleges* (Lexington: University Press of Kentucky, 1974), p. 24.

56. *Statistical Abstract*, 1953, p. 251.

57. For the loan provisions, see Davis R. B. Ross, *Preparing for Ulysses* (New York: Columbia University Press, 1969), p. 101. Under a 1945 amendment the Veterans Administration could pay tuition in excess of $500, but the veteran thereby suffered a proportionate reduction in his or her four years of eligibility.

58. *Statistical Abstract*, 1953, p. 236.

59. Sar A. Levitan and Karen A. Cleary, *Old Wars Remain Unfinished* (Baltimore: Johns Hopkins University Press, 1973), p. 1.

60. Olson, *G.I. Bill*, p. 44, table 1.

61. *Statistical Abstract*, 1977, p. 381, no. 620.

62. Levitan and Cleary, *Old Wars*, p. 125, table 23.

63. Quoted in Olson, *G.I. Bill*, p. 25.

64. Quoted in *ibid.*, p. 49.

65. However, the British, who ate unexpectedly well during the war, did not ration bread until after the war. See Mancur Olson, Jr., *The Economics of the Wartime Shortage* (Durham: Duke University Press, 1963), pp. 129–30.

66. Of course, gas rationing was imposed mainly to save rubber, not gasoline.

67. Polenberg, *War and Society*, p. 148.

68. Gerald D. Nash, *The Great Depression and World War II* (New York: St. Martin's Press, 1979), p. 147.

69. *Historical Statistics*, pt. 1, p. 373, ser. 506.

70. I. L. Kandel, *The Impact of the War upon American Education* (Chapel Hill: University of North Carolina Press, 1948), p. 88.

71. *Historical Statistics*, pt. 1, p. 372, ser. 446.

72. *Ibid.*, p. 378, ser. 575.

73. Raymond Walters, "Facts and Figures of Colleges at War," in *Higher Education and the War: The Annals of the American Academy of Political and Social Science*, January 1944, p. 8.

74. Kandel, *Impact of the War*, p. 160.

75. *Ibid.*, p. 126.

76. Faith M. Williams, "The Standard of Living in Wartime," *Annals of the American Academy of Political and Social Science* (September 1943), 229:117-27.

77. *Historical Statistics*, pt. 1, p. 85, ser. B-444–47.

78. In this calculation, wage and salary supplements, the growth of which was a striking wartime phenomenon that exceeded the percentage rise of wages and salaries, are excluded. "Real" means money compensation deflated by the consumer price index on a 1935–39 base. "Private" means nongovernmental. However, in calculating compensation per worker, the numerator contains agriculture but the denominator does not; this throws off the level of annual compensation, but probably not the percentage increases.

79. *Economic Report of the President*, January 14, 1948, p. 114, table VI.

80. *Historical Statistics*, pt. 1, p. 182, ser. 1029, 1030, 1035. In mining a declining trend continued during the war.

81. *Historical Statistics*, pt. 1, p. 483, ser. 260.

82. *Economic Report of the President*, January 14, 1948, p. 83.

83. *Historical Statistics*, pt. 1, p. 301, ser. G-319, 320, 323. Later figures are not strictly comparable, owing to a change in measurement techniques, but they are nonetheless indicative of a permanent shift:

	lowest 40%	highest fifth
1950	16.5%	42.7%
1960	17.0	41.3
1965	17.4	40.9
1970	17.6	40.9
1975	17.2	41.1
1979	16.9	41.6

Statistical Abstract, 1977, p. 443, no. 713, and 1981, p. 438, no. 730.

83. *Historical Statistics*, pt. 1, p. 301, ser. G-319, 320, 323.

84. Geoffrey H. Moore, "Secular Changes in the Distribution of Income," *American Economic Review* (May 1952), 42(2):528.

85. *Economic Report of the President*, January 1951, p. 49.

86. Selma F. Goldsmith, "Statistical Information on the Distribution of Income by Size in the United States," *American Economic Review* (May 1950), 40(2):334.

87. *Economic Report of the President*, January 14, 1948, p. 18.

88. On this point see also Moore, "Secular Changes," p. 540.

89. Edward C. Budd, "Postwar Changes in the Size Distribution of Income in the U.S.," *American Economic Review* (May 1970), 40(2):260.

8. The War's Consequences

1. Stanley Vance, *American Industries* (New York: Prentice-Hall, 1955), p. 221.

2. *1945 Collier's Year Book Covering the Events of the Year 1944* (New York: P. F. Collier & Son, 1945), pp. 94–98.

3. U.S. Congress, Senate Subcommittee on War Mobilization of the Committee on Military Affairs, *Wartime Technological Developments*, 79th Cong., 1st sess., Monograph no. 2 (May 1945), and Supplement for 1944 (Washington, D.C.: GPO, May and September 1945).

4. Samuel Rezneck, "Mass Production and the Use of Energy," in Harold F. Williamson, ed., *The Growth of the American Economy* (Englewood Cliffs, N.J.: Prentice-Hall, 1951), p. 733.

5. *Statistical Abstract*, 1982–83, p. 368, no. 617.

6. Portland *Oregonian*, June 3, 1984, p. A18.

7. Calculated from *Economic Report of the President*, February 1984, p. 220. The ratio was to continue to fall, e.g., it was running about 63 percent after the mid-fifties.

8. The explosion in domestic public transfer payments to persons, after the initial jump in veterans' transfers immediately following the war, did not occur until the late fifties. These transfers were an additional hallmark of the mixed economy.

9. The spread of the sales tax had already done a similar job on the state and local levels during the Great Depression.

10. Broadus Mitchell, *Depression Decade* (New York: Rinehart, 1947), p. 187.

11. *Economic Report of the President*, January 14, 1948, p. 82.

12. See U.S. Department of Agriculture, Agricultural Stabilization and Conservation Service, "Commodity Programs and Related Legislation Through the Years," BI no. 11, May 1976, pp. 3–5 *passim*.

13. *Economic Report of the President*, January 1953, p. 124.

14. See Martin Estey, *The Unions: Structure, Development, and Management*, 2d ed. (New York: Harcourt Brace Jovanovich, 1976), p. 113. Estey notes that this new intrusion of government was "looked upon with concern by the devotees of free (unregulated) collective bargaining on both sides of the table."

15. Of the 35 national emergency disputes settled under the act between 1947 and 1978, seven occurred in its very first year of labor management turmoil. U.S., Department of Labor Statistics, *National Emergency Disputes under the Taft-Hartley Act, 1947–77*, Report no. 542, November 1978, p. 1.

16. Gerard D. Reilly, "States Rights and the Law of Labor Relations," in Edward H. Chamberlin et al., *Labor Unions and Public Policy* (Washington, D.C.: American Enterprise Association, 1958), p. 109.

17. Mention should also be made of the 1958 Welfare and Pension Plans Disclosure Act, which required filing by union administration with the Secretary of Labor descriptions and

annual financial reports on all health, insurance, pension, and supplementary unemployment compensation plans.

18. U.S., Department of Labor, Bureau of Labor Statistics, *A Brief History of the American Labor Movement*, rev. ed., Bulletin no. 1000 (Washington, D.C.: GPO, 1970), pp. 124–25.

19. Lloyd G. Reynolds, *Labor Economics and Labor Relations*, 6th ed. (Englewood Cliffs, N.J.: Prentice-Hall, 1974), p. 604.

20. Washington University, Center for the Study of American Business, "A Decade of Rapid Growth in Federal Regulation" St. Louis, Mo., March 13, 1979, pp. 6–10, *passim*, table 2.

21. Various *Annual Reports* of the NLRB.

22. NLRB, *Annual Report* for 1959, p. 7, and for 1979, p. 29.

23. Using the federal purchases deflator.

24. Louis M. Kohlmeier, Jr., *The Regulators* (New York: Harper and Row, 1969), p. 247.

25. Cited in David E. Kaiser, *Economic Diplomacy and the Origins of the Second World War* (Princeton: Princeton University Press, 1980), p. 239. The French Premier Daladier spoke with similar alarm to the ambassador: "Into the battle zones, devastated and denuded of men, Cossack and Mongol hordes would then pour, bringing to Europe a new 'culture.' " *Ibid.*

26. Paul Y. Hammond, *The Cold War Years: American Foreign Policy Since 1945* (New York: Harcourt, Brace, and World, 1969), pp. 235–36.

27. The IMF did extend some financial and technical assistance to the LDCs. See Brian Tew, *The International Monetary Fund: Its Present Role and Future Prospects*, Princeton University, Department of Economics, Essays in International Finance, no. 36 (March 1961), pp. 4–6.

28. Including two subsequently created adjuncts to the IBRD, the International Finance Corporation (IFC, 1956) and the International Development Association (IDA, 1960), both designed to follow more liberal and more long-term loan policies toward the LDCs than the IBRD.

29. Eric Roll, *The World After Keynes* (New York: Praeger, 1968), p. 94.

30. See Leland B. Yeager, *International Monetary Relations* (New York: Harper and Row, 1966), p. 347.

31. *Ibid.*

32. Tew, *International Monetary Fund*, p. 13.

33. Delbert A. Snider, *International Monetary Relations* (New York: Random House, 1966), p. 100.

34. Frank A. Southard, Jr., *The Evolution of the International Monetary Fund*, Princeton University, Department of Economics, Essays in International Finance, no. 135 (December 1979), p. 25.

35. A. J. Youngson, *The British Economy 1920–1957* (Cambridge, Mass.: Harvard University Press, 1960), p. 167.

36. Edward M. Bernstein, "International Effects of U.S. Economic Policy," Study Paper no. 16, Joint Economic Committee, U.S. Congress, 86th Cong., 2d sess., January 25, 1960, p. 61.

37. Edward S. Mason and Robert E. Asher, *The World Bank Since Bretton Woods* (Washington, D.C.: Brookings Institution, 1973), p. 745.

38. Harry G. Johnson, *The World Economy at the Crossroads* (Montreal: Canadian Trade Committee, 1965), pp. 42, 43.

39. *Ibid.*, p. 10.

40. Quoted in Raymond Mikesell, "The Emergence of the World Bank as a Development Institution," in A. L. K. Acheson, J. F. Chant, and M. F. J. Prachowny, eds., *Bretton Woods Revisited* (Toronto: University of Toronto Press, 1972), p. 80.

41. Mason and Asher, *The World Bank Since Bretton Woods*, pp. 739, 741.

42. IBRD, *Fifteenth Annual Report, 1959–1960*, p. 12. By 1968, 80 percent of the aid of major industrial donors was tied (i.e., contained the requirement that recipients spend the aid funds in the donor country), and the proportion reached 98 percent in the case of the United States (Statement of Roberto de Oliveira Campos, president of the Inter-American Council of Trade and Production, *Hearings* before the Subcommittee on Foreign Economic Policy, Joint Economic Committee, 91st Cong., 1st sess., pt. 1, December 3, 1969, p. 92.

43. Alan S. Milward, *War, Economy, and Society* (Berkeley: University of California Press, 1977), p. 364.

44. Calculated from World Bank, *Annual Report*, 1976, p. 3.

45. A connection was formally acknowledged: the IMF governed trade restraints for balance-of-payments purposes. The Bretton Woods Conference admitted that the objectives of the IMF could not be achieved through the activities of the IMF alone.

46. Quoted in U.S., Senate, Committee on Finance, *Staff Analysis of Certain Issues Raised by the General Agreement on Tariffs and Trade*, 91st Cong., 2d sess., Committee Print, December 19, 1970, (Washington, D.C.: GPO, 1970), p. 2.

47. Raymond Vernon, *Trade Policy in Crisis*, Princeton University, Essays in International Finance, no. 29, March 1958, p. 4.

48. Gerald A. Pollack, "Perspectives on the United States International Financial Position," Staff Materials, Joint Economic Committee, U.S. Congress, 88th Cong., 1st sess. (Washington, D.C.: GPO, 1963), p. 33.

49. Johnson, *The World Economy at the Crossroads*, p. 32.

50. A former director of GATT argued in 1969, for example, that "the vast markets . . . opened up to exploitation by the great U.S. multinational companies whose foreign earnings are becoming an increasingly important factor in the U.S. balance of payments" attested to the fact that "the United States has done well out of the Community"; Statement of Eric Wyndham-White, in U.S. Congress, Joint Economic Committee, Subcommittee on Foreign Economic Policy, *Hearings*, pt. 1, December 3, 1969, p. 79 (Washington, D.C.: GPO, 1979).

51. See Committee on Finance, *Staff Analysis*, p. 3.

52. See, e.g., Statement of George A. Stinson, Chairman, American Iron and Steel Institute, before the Subcommittee on Foreign Economic Policy, Hearings, p. 70.

53. Committee on Finance, *Staff Analysis*, p. 4.

54. *Economic Report of the President*, February 1971, p. 154.

55. Peter B. Kenen, U.S. Congress, Joint Economic Committee, Subcommittee on Foreign Economic Policy, *Commercial Policy*, 87th Cong., 1st sess. (Washington, D.C.: GPO. 1961), p. 4.

56. *Economic Report of the President*, January 1967, p. 175.

57. Raymond Vernon, *America's Foreign Trade Policy and the GATT*, Princeton University, Essays in International Finance, no. 21, October 1954, p. 8.

58. Assar Lindbeck, "Economic Dependence and Interdependence in the Industrialized World," in Lincoln Gordon, ed., *From Marshall Plan to Global Interdependence* (Paris: Organization for Economic Cooperation and Development, 1978), p. 61.

59. *Ibid.*, pp. 61–62, 67.

60. Otmar Emminger (President of the Deutsche Bundesbank), "The Exchange Rate as an Instrument of Policy," *Lloyds Bank Review* (July 1979), 133:16–17, 20.

Index